Contents

Nature of economics 1
- Economics as a social science 1
- Positive vs. normative economic statements 1
- The economic problem 1
- Production Possibility Frontiers (PPF) 1
- Division of labour 2
- Comparing economists' views of markets 2
- Free market, mixed, and command economies 2

How markets work 3
- Rational decision-making 3
- Demand 3
- Elasticities of demand 4
- Supply 5
- Elasticity of supply 5
- Price determination 5
- Price mechanism 5
- Consumer and producer surplus 6
- Indirect taxes and subsidies 6
- Alternative views of consumer behaviour 6

Market failure 7
- Types of market failure 7
- Public goods 7
- Information gaps 7
- Externalities 7

Government intervention 8
- Government intervention in markets 8
- Government failure 9

Measures of economic performance 10
- Economic growth 10
- Inflation 10
- Employment and unemployment 11
- Balance of payments 11

Aggregate demand 12
- Characteristics of AD 12

Aggregate supply 13
- Characteristics of AS 13
- Short-run AS (SRAS) and long-run AS (LRAS) 13

National income 14
- Injections and withdrawals 14
- Equilibrium levels of real national output 14
- The multiplier 15

Economic growth 15
- Causes of economic growth 15
- Trade (business) cycle 15
- Output gaps 16
- Impact of economic growth 16

Macroeconomic objectives and policies 17
- Demand-side policies 17
- Macroeconomic objectives 17
- Government budget: deficit and surplus 17
- Direct and indirect taxation 17
- The role of the Bank of England 18
- Supply-side policies 18
- Conflicts and trade-offs between policies and objectives 19

Business growth and objectives 19
- Sizes and types of firms 19
- Business growth 20
- Demergers 20
- Business objectives 21

Revenue, costs, and profits 21
- Revenue 21
- Costs 22
- Normal profits, supernormal profits, and losses 22
- Economies and diseconomies of scale 22

Market structures 23
- Efficiency 23
- Perfect competition 23
- Monopolistic competition 24
- Oligopoly 24
- Monopoly 25
- Monopsony 26
- Contestability 26

Labour market 27
- Demand and supply of labour 27
- Wage determination in competitive/non-competitive markets 27
- Labour market interventions 27

Government intervention 28
- Government interventions 28

International economics 28
- Globalisation 28
- Specialisation and trade 29
- Patterns and terms of trade 29
- Trading blocs and the World Trade Organisation 30
- Restrictions on free trade 30
- Balance of payments 31
- Exchange rates 32
- International competitiveness 33

Poverty and inequality 33
- Absolute and relative poverty 33
- Inequality 33

Emerging and developing economies 34
- Measures of development 34
- Factors influencing growth and development 34
- Strategies influencing growth and development 35

The financial sector 36
- The financial sector 36

State role in macroeconomy 36
- National debt 36
- Public expenditure 36
- Public sector finances and fiscal deficit 36
- Taxation 37
- Macroeconomic policies in a global context 37

Nature of economics

Economics as a social science
- Economics is the study of how societies allocate scarce resources to satisfy people's needs and wants. Economists use models with assumptions to explain behaviour.
- The *ceteris paribus* assumption means all other things remain constant. Economists use this assumption to build models and focus on how one factors affects the other.
- Economics is a social science that involves people, so lab experiments are not possible. Policies may not work the same in every country.

Positive vs. normative economic statements
Models help predict outcomes but the assumptions behind models often reflect value judgements.

Positive economic statements	Normative economic statements
Based on facts and evidence	Based on value judgements
Can be proved or disproved	Cannot be proved or disproved
Objective	Subjective

The economic problem
Scarcity exists because wants are infinite, but resources are limited. Choices need to be made about what goods and services to produce (and how much), as well as how to produce and allocate them.

Factors of production:
- **Land:** natural resources (e.g. oil, water, raw materials)
- **Labour:** human effort (mental + physical)
- **Capital:** man-made tools used in production (e.g. machines, buildings)
- **Enterprise:** entrepreneurs who organise factors of production and take risks

Renewable vs. non-renewable resources:
- **Renewable resources:** naturally replaced over time; sustainable if not overused (e.g. solar energy, wind power).
- **Non-renewable resources:** finite and will eventually run out (e.g. oil, copper).

Opportunity cost: the value of the next best alternative that is given up.
- **Consumers:** choosing a laptop over a phone → phone is the opportunity cost
- **Producers:** investing in machinery over a factory → factory is the opportunity cost
- **Government:** building a hospital over a school → school is the opportunity cost

Production Possibility Frontiers (PPF)
A PPF shows the **maximum potential output** combinations of two goods/services an economy can produce when all resources are used efficiently.
- **Opportunity cost:** increasing the output of Good X means sacrificing some of Good Y
- **Efficient allocation:** any point on the curve (A, B, C) This means all resources are fully used.
- **Inefficient allocation:** any point inside the curve (E). This means some resources are unused (e.g. unemployed workers or unused machines).
- **Unattainable production:** points outside the curve (D) This is only possible with economic growth.
- **Movements along a PPF** represent a change in combination of two goods produced. For instance, by choosing to produce more of good X, quantity of good Y will decrease as more resources will be devoted to good X.
- Factors that can cause an **outward PPF shift**:
  ◦ Discovery of new natural resources
  ◦ Development of new methods that increase productivity
  ◦ Advances in technology and machinery.
  ◦ Better training
- Factors that can cause an **inward PPF shift**:
  ◦ Natural disasters that cause destruction
  ◦ Depletion of natural resources
  ◦ Factors that cause reduction in the size of the workforce

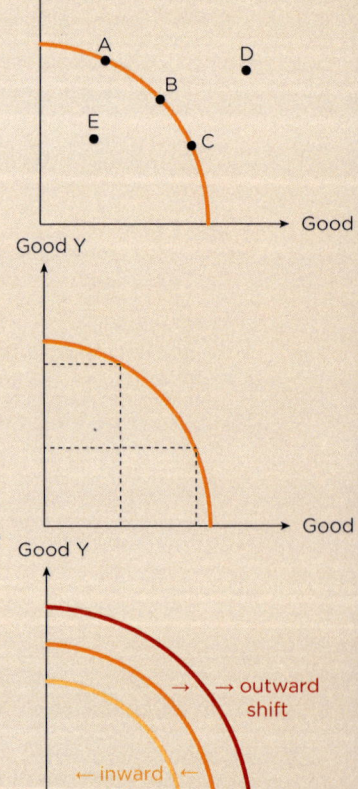

Capital and consumer goods
- **Capital goods:** used to produce other goods and services, but do not directly satisfy the consumer (e.g. machinery, tools, factories).
- **Consumer goods:** provide utility to consumers and are used directly by them for satisfaction (e.g. smartphones, clothes, cars).

Nature of economics

Division of labour
- Work is split into small, specialised tasks.
- Workers focus on specific jobs (e.g. in a bakery: one mixes dough, another bakes, another decorates).
- Father of economics **Adam Smith** described the division of labour as boosting economic growth by breaking tasks into smaller parts, meaning workers become experts without switching tasks.

Advantages	Disadvantages
Efficiency: higher quality and quantity production	Repetition and boredom: can lower productivity
Lower training costs: workers only learn one task	Limited skills: risky if workers lose jobs (harder to find new ones)
Time saving: less switching between jobs	Production disruption: strikes or absences can halt production

- **Specialisation in production and trade:** countries focus on producing goods they make most efficiently and trade these for others.

Advantages	Disadvantages
Increased output	Dependence on other countries
More variety of goods for consumers	Possible unemployment if industries shrink
Lower prices due to cost savings	Risk of trade deficits harming the economy

- **Limitations** to division of labour include **market size** (small markets limit specialisation) and **type of product** (niche/customised goods may be unsuitable).

Functions of money
Money enables specialisation and trade by acting as a
- **Medium of exchange** (trading goods/services)
- **Measure of value** (compare goods/services)
- **Store of value** (saving money for future purchases)
- **Method of deferred payment** (buy now, pay later/credit options).

Comparing economists' views of markets
- **Adam Smith:** believed self-interest benefits society and government's role should be limited to defence, justice, public goods.
- **Friedrich Hayek:** strong supporter of private property and believes that state planning limits freedom.
- **Karl Marx:** believed that the bourgeoisie exploit workers and predicted worker revolution which would lead to communism.

Free market, mixed, and command economies
- **Free market economy:**
  - Prices set by supply and demand, no government interference.
  - Resources are allocated by price mechanism.
  - Producers aim to maximise profits and consumers aim to maximise utility.
  - Resources are privately owned.

Advantages	Disadvantages
Consumer spending drives production	Resource owners can become richer, increasing inequality
Quick response to consumer needs	Monopolies can exploit consumers with high prices
Greater variety of goods and services	External costs and benefits often ignored

- **Command economy:**
  - Government allocates resources and sets prices.
  - Public ownership of resources.
  - Producers must meet state-set targets.
  - Aims for greater income and wealth equality.

Advantages	Disadvantages
Ensures a minimum standard of living for everyone	Lack of profit/competition may cause inefficiency
Externalities are managed in planning	Consumer preference is ignored
Prevents exploitation by monopolies	Slow response to changing consumer needs

- **Mixed economy:**
  - Combines free market and government allocation.
  - Most countries use this system.
  - Balance of market and state control varies by country.

Advantages	Disadvantages
Efficient resource allocation with social welfare, combining market efficiency with government intervention	Public sector intervention can lead to bureaucracy, waste, or inefficient allocation of resources
The state can provide essential services that a free market may underprovide (e.g. healthcare, education)	Taxes and regulations may reduce profit motives, limiting innovation and productivity
Government regulation and fiscal policy can help reduce inflation, unemployment, and economic volatility	Government decisions may be influenced by politics rather than economics, leading to suboptimal outcomes

How markets work

Rational decision-making

- **Consumers aim to maximise utility:**
  - Consumers are assumed to act rationally by choosing combinations of goods and services that provide the greatest satisfaction (utility) within their budget constraints.
  - Decisions are based on marginal utility per unit of cost.
  - The **equimarginal principle** suggests consumers allocate spending where utility per pound is equal across goods.
  - This assumes perfect information and logically ranked preferences.
- **Firms aim to maximise profits**
  - Firms are assumed to act rationally by choosing output levels and pricing strategies that maximise the difference between total revenue and total costs. Profit maximisation typically occurs where the **marginal cost (MC) = marginal revenue (MR)**.
  - This assumption underpins many models of firm behaviour, though in reality firms may also pursue goals like revenue maximisation, market share, or ethical objectives.

- **Movement along demand curve:** caused by a change in the price of the good itself (quantity demanded changes). For instance, when price decreases from P_1 to P_2, demand increases from Q_1 to Q_2. Conversely, when price increases from P_1 to P_3, demand decreases from Q_1 to Q_3.

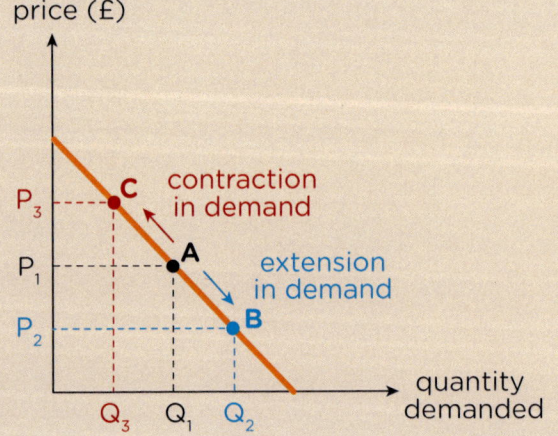

Demand

- Demand is the quantity of goods and services consumers are willing and able to buy at a certain price and time.
- **Diminishing marginal utility of demand:**
  - **Total utility:** satisfaction from total units consumed.
  - **Marginal utility:** satisfaction from one extra unit consumed.
  - **Law of diminishing marginal utility:** as more units are consumed, marginal utility decreases. This explains why consumers pay less for extra units and why demand curves slope downward.
- **Demand curve:** downward sloping due to the:
  - **Substitution effect:** if a good's price increases, consumers tend to buy cheaper alternatives.
  - **Income effect:** when prices rise, consumers' real income falls which will reduce quantity demanded.
- **Shifts in demand curve:** demand increases or decreases due to factors other than the good's price:
  - **Population:** more people → higher demand
  - **Advertising:** successful ads → demand rises
  - **Income:** higher real incomes → demand rises for most goods
  - **Substitutes and complements:**
    - Price rise in substitute → demand for this good increases (e.g. tea price increases → coffee demand increases).
    - Price fall in complement → demand for related good increases (e.g. printer price decreases → printer ink demand increases).

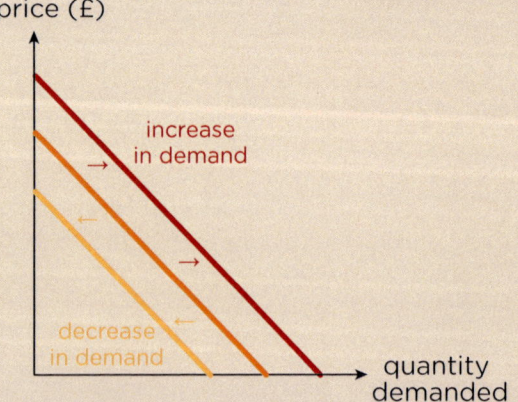

How markets work

Elasticities of demand

- **Price Elasticity of Demand (PED):** measures how much quantity demanded changes when the price changes.

$$PED = \frac{\% \text{ change in quantity demanded}}{\% \text{ change in price}}$$

  - Results:
    - Between 0 and −1 = **Price inelastic** (quantity demanded changes less than price)
    - Less than −1 = **Price elastic** (quantity demanded changes more than price)
    - Exactly −1 = **Unit elastic** (proportional change)
    - 0 = **Perfectly inelastic** (quantity demanded doesn't change at all)
    - Infinity = **Perfectly elastic** (quantity demanded changes infinitely with price change)
  - Factors influencing PED:
    - **Proportion of income spent:** higher proportion of income spent → more elastic demand.
    - **Nature of product:** addictive goods (e.g. alcohol, tobacco) → inelastic demand
    - **Durability:** long-lasting goods → elastic demand (don't buy often)
    - **Availability of substitutes:** more substitutes → more elastic demand
  - PED and revenue:
    - **Inelastic demand:** price increases → total revenue (TR) increases
    - **Elastic demand:** price increases → TR decreases
    - **Unit elastic:** price change → TR stays the same
    - **Perfectly inelastic:** price change → TR changes same way by the same amount
    - **Perfectly elastic:** price increases → TR drops to zero
  - Significance:
    - **Firms:** knowing the PED helps them to decide whether to raise or lower prices to maximise revenue.
    - **Consumers:** if demand is inelastic, price increases will reduce real income (less purchasing power).
    - **Government:** taxes on inelastic goods raise more tax revenue without cutting demand.

- **Cross Elasticity of Demand (XED):** measures how much the demand for one product (Product A) changes when the price of another product (Product B) changes.

$$XED = \frac{\% \text{ change in quantity demanded of product A}}{\% \text{ change in price of product B}}$$

  - Results:
    - **Positive XED (+):** products are substitutes.
    - **Negative XED (−):** products are complements
  - Significance: helps firms understand relationships between products, so they can price smartly.

- **Income Elasticity of Demand (YED):** measures how much the demand for a product changes when real income changes.

$$YED = \frac{\% \text{ change in quantity demanded}}{\% \text{ change in real income}}$$

  - Results:
    - **Positive YED (+):** product is a **normal** good; as people earn more, they buy more.
    - **Negative YED (−):** product is an **inferior** good; as income rises, demand falls.
  - Significance:
    - **Firms:** knowing if product is income elastic helps predict sales during booms and recessions and helps firms know when it is right to invest.
    - **Government:** helps government estimate and maximise tax revenue.

How markets work

Supply
- Supply is the amount of goods and services producers are willing and able to sell at a given price over a certain time.
- The supply curve slopes upwards meaning higher quantity is supplied at a higher price.
- **Movements along the curve:**
  - If price increases → quantity supplied increases (move up the curve).
  - If price decreases → quantity supplied decreases (move down the curve).
- **Shifts in supply curve:** shifts happen when something other than price changes supply:
  - **Cost of production:** if costs (wages, raw materials, rent) go up, supply shifts left.
  - **Productivity:** more output per worker → supply shifts to the right.
  - **Subsidies:** government grants lead to lower production costs → supply shifts right.

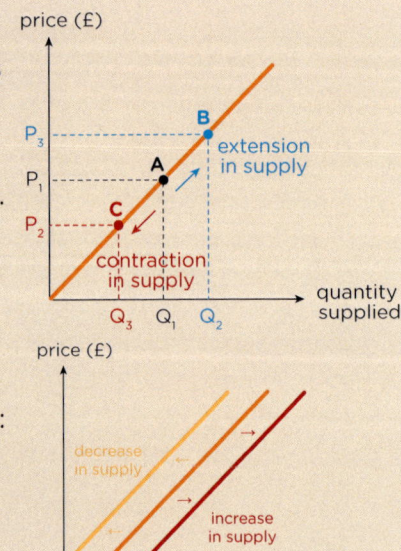

Elasticity of supply
- **Price Elasticity of Supply (PES):** measures how much the quantity supplied of a product changes when its price changes.

$$PES = \frac{\% \text{ change in quantity supplied}}{\% \text{ change in price}}$$

  - **Results:**
    - Always positive because supply curves slope upwards.
    - **Price Inelastic Supply:** 0 < PES < 1, supply changes less than price.
    - **Price Elastic Supply:** PES > 1, supply changes more than price change
    - **Unit Elastic Supply:** PES = 1, supply changes exactly as price change.
    - **Perfectly Inelastic Supply:** PES = 0, quantity supplied doesn't change.
    - **Perfectly Elastic Supply:** PES = infinity, any price change causes infinite change in quantity supplied.
  - **Factors influencing PES:**
    - **Short run:** at least one factor of production is fixed → harder to change supply → inelastic supply.
    - **Long run:** all factors variable → easy to adjust supply → more elastic supply.
    - **Spare capacity:** if a firm has unused machines or workers (spare capacity), it can increase supply quickly when price rises, resulting in elastic supply. If there is no spare capacity, supply tends to be inelastic.

Price determination
- In a free market, prices are set by the interaction of demand and supply.
- At equilibrium, sellers are happy with the amount they are selling and buyers maximise their satisfaction (utility).
- **Equilibrium:** occurs when demand = supply. The equilibrium price is called the market clearing price because sellers sell all stock without surplus or shortage. Any price above or below this creates disequilibrium.
- **Disequilibrium:**
  - **Excess demand (shortage):** when demand is greater than supply often because prices are too low.
    - Sellers sell out quickly at low prices.
    - Some buyers can't buy the product.
    - Sellers increase prices to increase profits.
    - As prices rise, quantity demanded falls and quantity supplied rises.
    - Over time, this restores equilibrium at a higher price and quantity.
    - Excess demand is $Q_d Q_s$.
  - **Excess supply (surplus):** when supply is greater than demand often because prices are too high.
    - Sellers can't sell.
    - Buyers can't buy as prices are too high.
    - Sellers lower prices to sell more.
    - As prices fall, quantity supplied decreases and quantity demanded increases.
    - Over time, this restores equilibrium at a lower price and quantity.
    - Excess supply is $Q_s Q_d$.

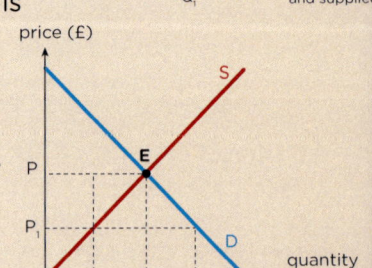

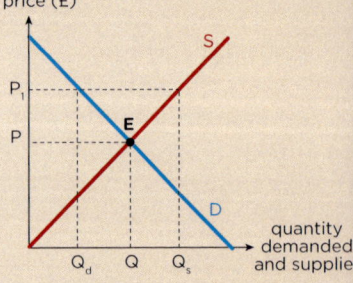

Price mechanism
The functions of the price mechanism to allocate resources include:
- **Signalling:** prices send signals to everyone in the market.
- **Incentive:** higher prices = bigger profits, motivating firms to produce more
- **Rationing:** when there's limited supply, prices rise which ration demand. Only people willing to pay that price get the goods. This keeps demand and supply balanced.

How markets work

Consumer and producer surplus
- **Consumer surplus:** the difference between the highest price a consumer is willing to pay and the actual price they pay. Consumer surplus is the area above the price line and below the demand curve (PEC).
- **Producer surplus:** the difference between the lowest price a producer is willing to accept and the price they receive. Producer surplus is the area below the price line and above the supply curve (PEA).

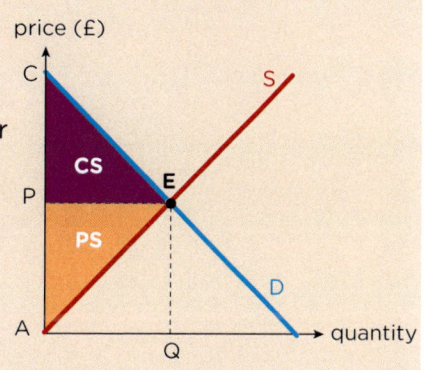

Alternative views of consumer behaviour
- **Bounded rationality:** consumers have limited cognitive ability, time, and information, leading to satisficing rather than optimal decisions.
- **Bounded self-control:** consumers may lack the willpower to act in their long-term interest (e.g. overconsumption, addiction).
- **Social norms:** behaviour is influenced by social expectations and peer pressure, not just individual preferences.
- **Altruism and fairness:** consumers may make choices based on fairness or to benefit others, rather than pure self-interest.
- **Habitual behaviour:** past consumption patterns strongly influence future choices, often regardless of price or utility.

Indirect taxes and subsidies
- **Indirect taxes** are taxes on goods or services paid when consumers buy them. They are usually placed on demerit goods to reduce demand and raise government revenue.
  ◦ The tax cost is shared between consumers and producers.
    - If demand is price inelastic, consumers pay most of the tax.
    - If demand is price elastic, producers pay most of the tax.
  ◦ Taxes shift the supply curve left (upwards), increasing price and reducing quantity sold.
    - P_1 and Q_1 is equilibrium.
    - Indirect tax causes supply curve to shift from S_1 to S_2.
    - Price increases from P_1 to P_2.
    - Consumer burden = P_1P_2AB.
    - Producer burden = EP_1BC.
    - Tax revenue to government = EP_2AC.

- **Subsidies** are payments by the government to producers to encourage production and consumption of merit goods.
  ◦ Subsidies shift the supply curve to the right, indicating an increase in supply as producers face lower production costs.
    - P_1 and Q_1 are equilibrium
    - After subsidy, new price falls to P_2.
    - Quantity rises to Q_2.
    - BC is subsidy.
    - Total cost of subsidy to government = P_2ABC.

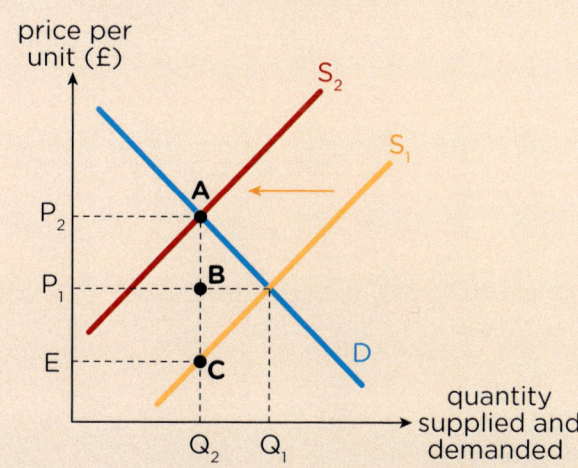

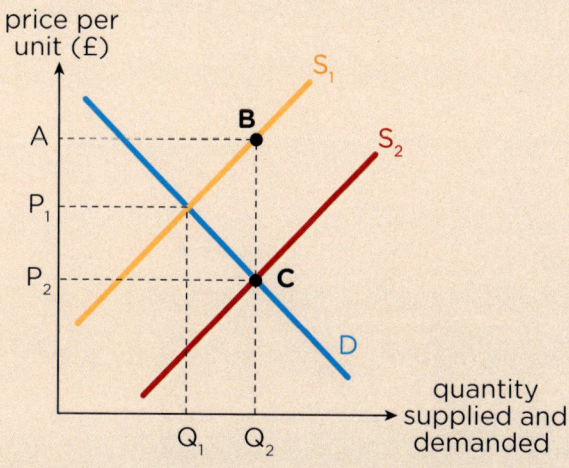

Market failure

Types of market failure

Market failure occurs when the market system fails to allocate resources efficiently, leading to a loss of economic and social welfare. Types of market failure include:
- **Externalities:** costs or benefits to third parties who are not involved in the transaction between producers and consumers.
- **Under-provision of public goods:** when the free market does not supply public goods in sufficient quantities.
- **Information gaps:** when consumers or producers lack sufficient information to make informed decisions.

Public goods

Public goods benefit many people. They have two main features:
- **Non-rivalrous:** one person's use doesn't reduce availability for others.
- **Non-excludable:** if one person can use it, everyone can.

By contrast, private goods are **rivalrous** and **excludable**.

Public goods are also subject to the **free-rider problem** whereby someone can benefit from a public good without paying for it. This causes market failure since not enough people want to pay, so it is unprofitable for businesses to supply.

Information gaps

- **Symmetric information:** both parties have equal information in a transaction.
- **Asymmetric information:** one party knows more than the other.
- This imbalance means one side might lack enough info to make rational choices, leading to inefficient resource allocation and market failure.

Externalities

Externalities are the benefits or costs experienced by third parties who are not directly involved in the economic transaction.
- **External costs (negative externalities):** are costs to third parties not involved in the transaction.
- **Private costs:** are costs paid directly by the consumer and producer in a transaction.
- **Social costs:** external costs + private costs
- **External costs of production:**
  - **Private Marginal Benefit (PMB):** is the demand curve and shows the benefit that consumers get from consuming one more unit of a good. As people consume more, the benefit they get from each extra unit falls. When we assume that there are no external benefits, PMB = Social Marginal Benefit (SMB).
  - **Private Marginal Cost (PMC):** is the supply curve and shows the cost to producers of making one more unit. As output rises, the cost of producing each extra unit increases. In a free market, the equilibrium output is where: PMB = PMC. This level of output is called A. However, A is not socially optimal as it doesn't consider external costs of production.
  - **Social Marginal Cost (SMC):** this curve adds private costs and external costs together. The socially optimal output is where: SMC = SMB. This level of output is called B. In a free market, the output is higher than optimal (overproduction and overconsumption of AB). This causes a welfare loss shown as area XYZ on the diagram.
- **External benefits (positive externalities):** are benefits to third parties not involved in a transaction.
- **Private benefits:** are benefits received directly by producer and consumer in a transaction.
- **Social benefits:** external benefits + private benefits
- **External benefits of consumption:**
  - **Private Marginal Benefit (PMB):** is the demand curve and shows the private benefits consumers get from consuming each extra unit. As consumption increases, these benefits decrease.
  - **Private Marginal Cost (PMC):** is the supply curve and shows the private costs to producers of making each extra unit. It's assumed there are no external costs so PMC = Social Marginal Cost (SMC). In a free market, the equilibrium output is where: PMB = PMC, which gives output level A. However, output A is not socially optimal because it does not include any external benefits of production.
  - **Social Marginal Benefit (SMB):** this curve includes both private benefits and external benefits. It lies to the right of the PMB curve because external benefits increase total benefit to society. The socially optimal output is where: SMC = SMB, which gives output level B. This means the free market produces too little output and consumption by amount BA. If output is increased to the socially optimal level B, society gains a welfare benefit (area ABC).

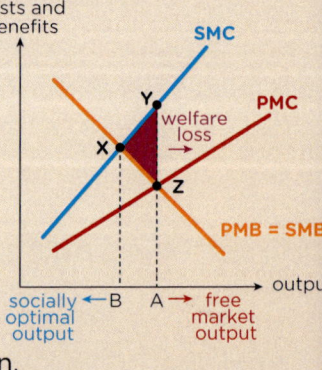

Government intervention

Government intervention in markets

- **Indirect taxes:** there are two different types of taxes: **ad valorem tax** (percentage of the price of the product) and **specific tax** (set amount per unit of the product).
  - Government can introduce indirect taxes to deal with external costs.
  - Indirect taxes help to internalise the externality.
  - Output and consumption move to the level at which SMB=SMC.
  - Tax causes supply curve to shift to left.
  - Consumption falls to B (socially optimal level).
  - Externality has been internalised.

Advantages	Disadvantages
Low administrative costs	Business costs increase
Governments gain tax revenue	Difficulty setting appropriate tax due to problem of quantifying external cost

- **Subsidies:** grants to businesses that help to reduce production costs. This means that the good or service can be provided at a lower price to encourage consumption of a product which has external benefits.
  - Subsidy causes supply to shift to the right.
  - Subsidy will cause consumption and output to increase from A to B
  - Socially optimal level is reached

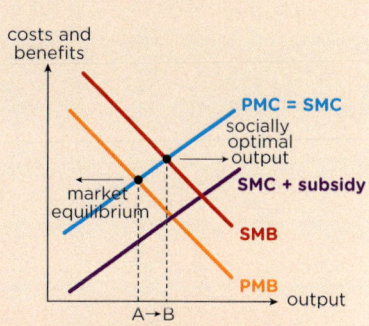

Advantages	Disadvantages
Lower price acts as an incentive for consumers to increase consumption	If demand is inelastic, subsidy is ineffective
Can help to reduce inequality	Difficult to set appropriate subsidy due to the problem of quantifying external benefit

- **Maximum prices/price ceilings:** are set by the government and mean firms have to charge more than the given price for a product.
  - Equilibrium is $Q_e P_e$
  - Government sets maximum price of P_{max}
  - There is a shortage of $Q_d Q_s$

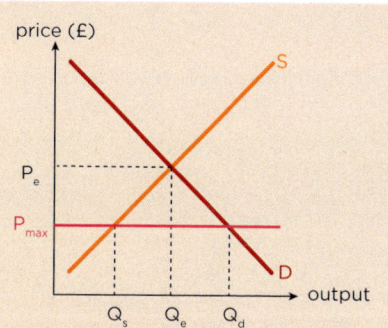

Advantages	Disadvantages
Enables consumers on low incomes to buy a product	Shortages mean that some consumers are unable to buy the product
Prevents exploitation of consumers by monopolies	Shortages could cause people to buy from black markets at prices that are significantly higher

- **Minimum prices:** are set by the government which is guaranteed to producers.
  - Equilibrium is $Q_e P_e$
  - Government sets minimum price of P_{min}
  - There is a surplus of supply ($Q_d Q_s$)
  - Government can buy this surplus and store it to sell when there is a shortage.

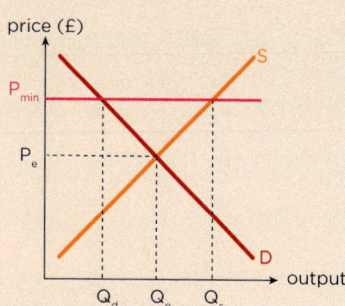

Advantages	Disadvantages
Producers know in advance the price they will get for a product	Minimum prices encourage over-production and could result in inefficient allocation of resources
Greater certainty allows producers to plan investment and output	Cost of storage has to be paid by taxpayers

Government intervention

Government intervention in markets (continued)

- **Tradable pollution permits:** are government policy used to control pollution by issuing permits that allow firms to pollute up to a set limit. Firms must pay fines if they exceed this limit. Permits can also be bought and sold between firms creating incentive for reducing pollution.

Advantages	Disadvantages
Uses market forces to reduce pollution	Pollution still occurs, just at controlled levels
Provides financial incentive for firms to cut pollution	Large firms can swallow the cost of extra permits and keep polluting
Allows for planned, gradual reduction of pollution over time	Can make domestic goods less competitive internationally

- **State provision of public goods:** when the free market fails to provide public goods, the government steps in to supply them, financing the provision through taxation.

Advantages	Disadvantages
Ensures that essential public goods or services exist	Government decides resource allocation without direct consumer input
Overcomes the free-rider problem, ensuring efficient funding through taxation	Can lead to government failure due to inefficiency or misallocation of resources

- **Provision of information:** government or agencies provide information to close information gaps, using publications online or printed materials to inform consumers about goods and services.

Advantages	Disadvantages
Helps consumers make better-informed decisions	Costs involved in producing and distributing information
Can reduce market failures caused by asymmetric information	No guarantee the policy will be effective

- **Regulation:** legal rules imposed on consumers and producers to control activities such as banning goods, limiting production processes, or restricting consumption (e.g. age limits).

Advantages	Disadvantages
Can reduce negative externalities and correct market failures, protecting consumers (e.g. enforcing safety standards)	Firms may face higher costs due to administrative burdens or changes to processes
Can prevent exploitation and ensure minimum standards (e.g. working conditions, anti-discrimination laws)	Poorly designed or overly strict regulations can distort markets or lead to unintended consequences
Can limit the amount of pollution	Enforcement of laws and regulations costs
Provides incentive for producers to develop new technology	Difficult to determine the socially efficient level of pollution

Government failure

Government failure occurs when government intervention in a market intended to correct a market failure results in a more inefficient allocation of resources causing a net welfare loss. The primary causes of government failure are:

- **Distortion of price signals:** government intervention manipulates prices, undermining the functions (signalling, rationing, and incentive) of the price mechanism, leading to inefficient resource allocation.
- **Unintended consequences:** interventions can have unexpected effects, e.g. high cigarette taxes leading to increased smuggling, reducing tax revenue.
- **Excessive administration costs:** the costs of enforcing and managing interventions can be very high, reducing overall efficiency.
- **Information gaps:** governments often lack complete information, causing interventions to push output further from the socially optimal level.

Measures of economic performance

Economic growth
- **GDP:** total value of goods and services produced in a country within one year. It can also represent total spending or total income. Increase in GDP signals economic growth.
- **Recession:** occurs when there are two consecutive quarters of negative economic growth. In a recession, spending, income, and output fall, causing business closures, higher unemployment, and lower living standards.
- **Nominal vs. real GDP:**
  - **Nominal GDP:** value of goods/services produced in a year at current prices.
  - **Real GDP:** nominal GDP adjusted for inflation, which allows us to track changes in actual output volume over time.
- **Total vs. per capita GDP:**
  - **Total GDP:** measures the overall economic output of a country within a given time period.
  - **Per capita GDP:** divides total GDP by the population, showing average income or output per person
- **Value vs. volume of output:**
  - **Volume:** the quantity of goods produced.
  - **Value:** quantity multiplied by the price at which the goods were sold.
- **GNI (Gross National Income):** total income earned by a country's residents, both domestically and from overseas net income.
- **Comparing growth rates between countries:** GDP helps compare living standards over time and across countries. Living standards include income and quality of life factors like housing, health, environment, and safety.
- **Purchasing Power Parities (PPP):** used to compare GDP across countries by accounting for the cost of a standard basket of goods in each country. The PPP exchange rate equalises purchasing power by removing price differences between countries.
- **Limits of GDP:**
  - Differences in population mean GDP per capita is a better comparison.
  - Inflation varies between countries, so real GDP (adjusted for inflation) must be used.
  - Exchange rate fluctuations affect comparisons.
  - Income distribution varies which GDP doesn't reflect.
- **National happiness:** the UK government runs regular surveys on personal wellbeing, estimating life satisfaction and tracking whether people find their lives meaningful. These measures relate to health, relationships, and employment, capturing subjective happiness and quality of life.
- **Real incomes vs. subjective happiness:** research shows income and happiness increase together, but only up to a point. After that, extra income brings smaller boosts to happiness. This is called the **Easterlin Paradox**.

Inflation
- **Inflation:** sustained increase in overall price level of goods/services.
- **Deflation:** sustained decrease in the general price level of goods/services.
- **Disinflation:** slowdown in the rate of inflation (prices rising, but slower).
- **Consumer Price Index (CPI):** how the UK measures inflation. The CPI shows the average price change of a basket of goods/services vs. a base year.
  - **CPI calculation:** survey of about 7,000 UK households who record all their purchases. CPI doesn't include housing costs like rent or mortgages.
    - Prices are collected for 700 commonly bought items.
    - Each item is weighted by cost vs. average household income.
    - Price changes are multiplied by these weights to create a price index.
  - **Limitations of CPI:**
    - Excludes housing costs, which are a big cost to most people.
    - Doesn't reflect spending patterns of all households.
    - Basket of 700 items is updated only once a year, so sudden changes aren't captured immediately.
- **Retail Price Index (RPI):** alternative measure of the rate of inflation. Includes mortgage interest payments but is less reliable than CPI or CPIH, especially for comparing internationally.
- **Causes of inflation:**
  - **Demand-pull inflation:** occurs when aggregate demand grows faster than aggregate supply. This is caused by: lower interest rates, higher business and consumer confidence, increased government spending, or depreciation of the exchange rate.
  - **Cost-push inflation:** occurs when aggregate supply decreases. This is caused by: rising oil or raw material prices, falling exchange rate, higher business taxes, rising wages, or increased regulations.
  - **Growth of money supply:** some economists (monetarists) say inflation is mainly caused by too much money circulating which increases AD.
- **Effects of inflation:**
  - **On consumers:** fixed income earners lose purchasing power (real income falls); savings lose value over time; loans become easier to pay off if inflation exceeds loan interest rates.
  - **On firms:** exports suffer if UK inflation is higher than trading partners, making UK goods expensive abroad and imports cheaper. High inflation also complicates budgeting and can reduce investment. Cost-push inflation reduces profits, lowering investment potential. Some inflation can help firms raise revenues.
  - **On government:** inflation lowers the real value of debt, making it easier to manage, increasing inequality since people on fixed incomes lose out.
  - **On workers:** those with weak bargaining power may see wages rise slower than inflation reducing real income.

Measures of economic performance

Employment and unemployment

- **Measures of unemployment:**
  - **Claimant count:** counts people claiming unemployment benefits (Jobseeker's Allowance/Universal Credit).
  - **Labour Force Survey (LFS):** surveys sample of households, asking if people have been out of work in the past 4 weeks and ready to start in 2 weeks. Uses International Labour Organisation (ILO) standards.
- **Unemployment vs. underemployment:**
  - **Unemployment:** percentage of labour force without a job but actively seeking work.
  - **Underemployment:** includes people wanting or available for more work.
- **Significance of changes in the rates of:**
  - **Employment:** increase in employment rate boosts GDP (increased output), raises incomes (better living standards) and increases tax revenue.
  - **Unemployment:** decreased unemployment cuts government spending on benefits but can make job markets less flexible (fewer workers to choose from).
  - **Inactivity:** economically inactive refers to those not looking for work and not unemployed (full-time students, carers and sick people etc.) Higher inactivity means less productive capacity, more welfare claims and higher proportion of population being dependent.
- **Causes of unemployment:**
  - **Structural:** declining industries and outdated skills.
  - **Frictional:** people who are switching jobs.
  - **Seasonal:** jobs lost during specific times (seasons) of the year.
  - **Demand-deficient (cyclical):** low spending means fewer jobs.
  - **Real wage inflexibility:** labour supply issues like minimum wages set too high which prevents adjustment.
- **Significance of migration and skills for employment and unemployment:**
  - **Migration:** people moving between countries. If immigrants fill job vacancies, employment rises. If they can't find work, unemployment increases.
  - **Skills:** skilled workforce matters because more productive workers boost economic growth, skilled workers usually earn more than unskilled ones, and skilled workers are less likely to be unemployed.
- **Effects of unemployment:**
  - **On consumers:** living standards drop, confidence and spending fall, and house prices fall which can reduce personal wealth.
  - **On firms:** easier to hire since more workers are available, and less consumer spending cuts sales, revenue, and profits.
  - **On workers:** skills can deteriorate, income loss may occur (as benefits aren't as high as wages), and lower living standards due to less money. Long-term unemployment (loss of skills) also makes job hunting harder.
  - **On government and society:** welfare spending increases (unemployment benefits), tax revenue falls as incomes drop, and inequality rises.

Balance of payments

Balance of payments is the record of all international payments over a year.
- The components of the balance of payments are:
  - **Current account:** Payments for transactions during the year. Includes:
    - **Balance of trade:** exports of goods minus imports of goods.
    - **Trade in services:** exports of services minus imports of services.
    - **Primary income:** earnings from foreign investments minus payments to foreigners.
    - **Secondary income:** transfers like money or goods (e.g. aid).
  - **Capital and finance accounts:** track investments and loans.
- A **current account surplus** means net trade balance is positive, so more money flows into the country than out.
- A **current account deficit** means net trade balance is negative, so more money flows out the country than in.
- **Relationship between current account imbalances and other macroeconomic objectives:**
  - A constant current account deficit can mean a country's goods aren't competitive.
  - This might cause unemployment to rise.
  - Economic growth could slow down.
  - Country's currency might fall compared to others.
  - Weaker currency makes imports more expensive.
  - Inflation increases.
- **Interconnectedness of economics through international trade:**
  - Countries depend on each other because of trade.
  - This helps cut costs and encourages cooperation.
  - However, trade blocs can form and get powerful.
  - This can end up blocking fair trade for developing countries.

Aggregate demand

Characteristics of AD

- **Aggregate Demand (AD):** total planned spending on goods and services in a country at a given price level over a year, given by **AD=C+I+G+(X-M)**.
- The components of AD are: **consumption (C):** ~60% (most significant component); **government spending (G):** ~25%; **investment (I):** ~15%; and **net trade (exports minus imports, X-M):** usually small impact.
- Reasons for the AD curve's downwards slope:
  - **Real balance effect:** when price levels increase, purchasing power falls which leads to decrease in demand for real output.
  - **International trade effect:** rise in price level, causes decrease in international competitiveness of UK's goods and services, increasing demand for imports which results in AD contracting.
  - **Interest rate effect:** high price level causes increased demand for money. This reduces consumption and investment and causes contraction in AD.
- **Movements along AD curve:** if price level falls from P_1 to P_2, then there is an extension in AD and real GDP also increases from G_1 to G_2. If price level rises from P_1 to P_3, AD contracts and real GDP falls from G_1 to G_3.
- **Shifts in AD curve:** AD shifts when one of the components changes. If AD increases, AD shifts to the right (AD to AD_1). AD is higher at each price level. If AD decreases, AD shifts to the left (AD to AD_2). AD is lower at each price level.

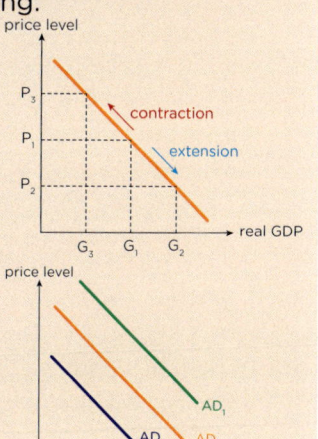

Consumption (C)

Consumption is the spending by households on goods and services. The key determiner of consumption is disposable income (DI) which is the money left after taxes to spend or save.
- **Savings vs. consumption:** money not spent assumed to be saved.
  - **Average Propensity to Consume (APC):** proportion of DI that is spent on goods and services, given by **consumption ÷ DI × 100**.
  - **Average Propensity to Save (APS):** proportion of DI saved, given by **savings ÷ DI × 100**. The APC + APS always equals 100%.
- **Influences on consumer spending** include **interest rates** (if borrowing is more expensive, people tend to spend less), **consumer confidence** (if people feel secure enough to splurge on goods/services), and the **wealth effect:** if house prices/stocks go up, people feel richer/spend more.

Investment (I)

- **Gross investment** = net investment + depreciation
- **Net investment** = gross investment − depreciation
- **Depreciation** is the wear and tear or loss in value of capital goods.
- **Influences on investment:**
  - **Rate of economic growth:** when real GDP goes up, firms need more machines and factories etc. to keep up → investment rises → more GDP growth → even more investment (multiplier).
  - **Business expectations and confidence:** if firms think sales will rise they're more likely to invest. If confidence is high, so is investment.
  - **Keynes' Animal Spirits:** describes the gut feeling or moods of business owners and whether they feel optimistic enough to invest.
  - **Demand for exports:** when foreign demand for a country's goods increases firms are likely to invest more; exporting may be complicated by regulations.
  - **Interest rates:** higher interest rates means that borrowing costs more → investment usually falls. Low interest rates don't always mean easy loans though as banks may be more hesitant to lend.
  - **Access to credit:** banks might not lend much if they think investment is risky even if interest rates are low.
  - **Influence of government and regulations:** changes in taxes, relaxed laws or incentives can push firms to invest more.

Government Expenditure (G)

- Influences on government expenditure:
  - **Trade cycle:** the economy may be in **downturn (recession):** GDP falls, unemployment rises → government spends more on welfare benefits, or a **boom (growth):** economy is strong → government spends less on benefits since fewer people need support.
  - **Fiscal policy:** governments control total spending in the economy by adjusting their own spending levels. This is called discretionary fiscal policy.

Net Trade (X − M)

- **Net trade** = value of exports − value of imports. The UK usually has a **negative net trade value** (i.e. it imports more than it exports).
- **Influences on net trade balance** include **real income** (when people earn more at home, they buy more local goods → less incentive for firms to export), **exchange rate** (if the pound gets stronger, UK exports get pricier for other countries → exports fall), the **state of the world economy** (if economies boom, demand for UK exports increases.), **degree of protectionism** (tariffs and trade restrictions make exporting harder), and **non-price factors** (e.g. quality, design, and shipping costs also affect export/import demand).

Aggregate supply

Characteristics of AS
- **Aggregate supply (AS):** total amount of goods and services that all firms in the economy are willing to supply at a given price level in an economy in a year. The AS curve is upwards sloping since as the general price level increases, real GDP will also increase.
- **Movements along AS curve:**
  - Movements along the AS curve happen when there are changes in price level which are not related to AS.
  - If there is an increase in consumption (AD), an extension in AS will occur and price level will increase from P_1 to P_2 and GDP will increase from G_1 to G_2.
  - If there is a decrease in AD, AS will contract and price level will fall from P_1 to P_3.

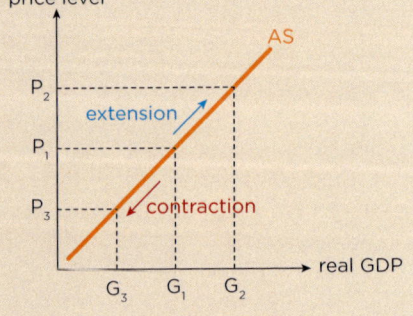

- **Shifts of AS curve:**
  - Shifts in AS curve are caused by changes in the cost of production.
  - If the cost of production increases, then AS will shift to the left (upwards) (AS to AS_2).
  - If the cost of production decreases, then AS will shift to the right (downwards) (AS to AS_1).

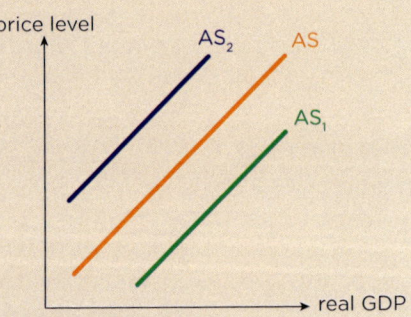

Short-run AS (SRAS)
SRAS is the **total output** firms are willing to produce at different price levels in the **short term**. The factors influencing SRAS include:
- **Raw material costs:** If prices of raw material rise, it costs more to produce. SRAS shifts left (decreases). If raw material costs fall, SRAS shifts right (increases).
- **Exchange rate changes:** If pound gets stronger, imports cost less → production becomes cheaper → SRAS shifts right.
- **Tax rates:** Lower taxes for firms mean lower costs → SRAS shifts right. Higher taxes pushes costs up → SRAS shifts left.

Long-run AS (LRAS)
LRAS shows the economy's **maximum sustainable output.** Factors that influence LRAS include:
- **Technological advances:** new technology makes production more efficient → LRAS shifts right.
- **Relative productivity:** if workers get more output per hour (better tools, training, motivation) → LRAS shifts right
- **Education and skills:** more skilled workforce = more productive economy → LRAS shifts right.
- **Government and regulations:** laws that slow production or force costly changes → LRAS shifts left. Regulations that encourage innovation or competition → LRAS shift right.
- **Demographic changes and migration:** more working-age people or skilled immigrants means more supply → LRAS shifts right. Aging population or fewer workers → LRAS shifts left.
- **Competition policy:** government makes it easier to start and run businesses → encourages production/innovation → LRAS shifts right.

Relationship between SRAS and LRAS
- **SRAS:** assumes some resources are fixed.
- **LRAS:** there are two types of LRAS curves:
  - **Classical view:** LRAS can be drawn as vertical line as it is perfectly inelastic. This means a shift in AD has no impact on the output since AS curve is perfectly inelastic in long run if the country is in equilibrium.
  - **Keynesian view:** LRAS curve can be drawn as a backwards sloping L.
    - Output can be increased without significant increase in costs.
    - There is spare capacity due to unused resources in the economy.
    - An economy can be in equilibrium and also have spare capacity.

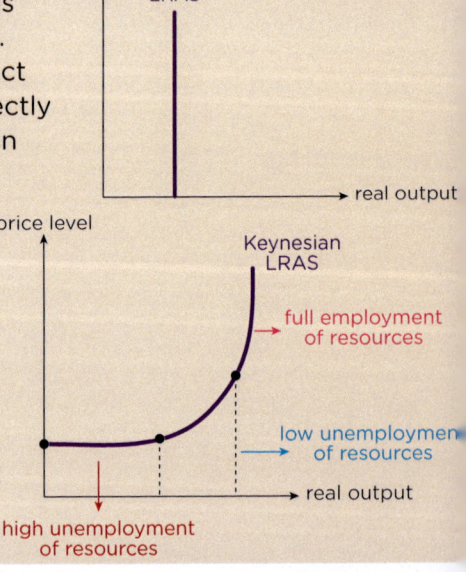

National income

National income

National income is the total value of all goods and services produced by a country in a year.

- **Circular flow of income:**
  - Households provide factors of production (land, labour etc.).
  - In return, they receive factor payments (wages, rent).
  - They then spend this money to buy goods and services.
- **Income and wealth:**
  - **Wealth:** total value of everything owned by a person, company, or country, measured at a specific time.
  - **Income:** money earned over a period from work, investments, or other sources, measured over a period of time.

Injections and withdrawals

Injections: money added into the economy.
- **Investment (I):** when businesses spend money to grow their operations.
- **Government spending (G):** when government buys goods and services or provides benefits.
- **Exports (X):** when other countries buy goods or services made in your country. This brings money in.

Withdrawals (leakages): money taken out of the economy.
- **Savings (S):** when people put money aside instead of spending it now.
- **Taxes (T):** money paid to the government that is taken out of people's spending.
- **Imports (M):** when people buy goods or services from other countries, sending money out.

If injections > withdrawals, more money flows through the economy and it grows.
If withdrawals > injections, less money is spent and the economy can shrink.

Equilibrium levels of real national output

- Equilibrium point is when AD intersects AS curve.
- There is no reason for price level to change at equilibrium point.
- If price level was higher than P_e, there would be a tendency for it to fall.
- If price level was lower than P_e, there would be shortages and price level would start to rise.
- **Shifts in curves:**
  - If AS decreases → AS curve shifts to the left ($AS_1 → AS_2$).
    - Equilibrium price increases $P_1 → P_2$
    - Output decreases $O_1 → O_2$.
  - If AD increases → AD shifts to the right ($AD_1 → AD_2$).
    - Equilibrium price increases $P_1 → P_2$.
    - Output increases $O_1 → O_2$.
    - Depends on the elasticity of the AS curve.
  - If it is perfectly inelastic (classical), there will be no effect on real output.
  - There will be a higher effect on output than price level if curve is elastic.

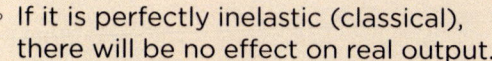

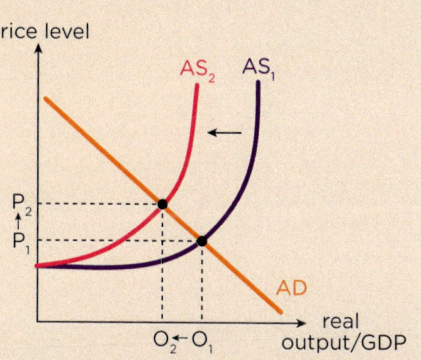

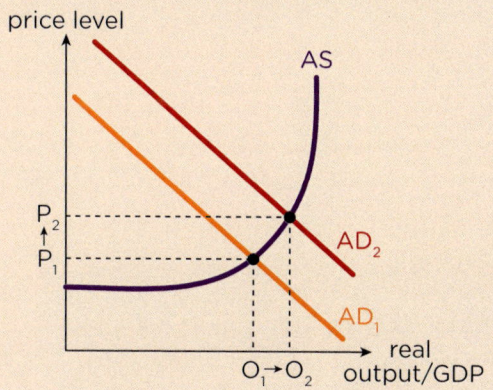

Economic growth

The multiplier

The multiplier shows how much total income (GDP) changes in response to a change in injections or withdrawals in the economy.

$$\text{Multiplier (K)} = \frac{\text{change in real GDP}}{\text{change in injections}}$$

When an injection enters the economy, it doesn't just increase GDP by that amount – the total effect is bigger because initial spending leads to more spending by others. This magnifies the impact on the economy.

- **Marginal propensities that affect the multiplier:**
  - **Marginal Propensity to Consume (MPC):** proportion of extra income that people spend on goods and services.

    $$MPC = \frac{\text{change in consumption}}{\text{change in income}}$$

    $$\text{Multiplier} = \frac{1}{1 - MPC}$$

  - **Marginal Propensity to Save (MPS):** proportion of extra income saved.

    $$MPS = \frac{\text{change in savings}}{\text{change in income}}$$

    $$\text{Multiplier} = \frac{1}{MPS}$$

  - **Marginal Propensity to Tax (MPT):** proportion of extra income paid as taxes. When MPT increases, multiplier decreases because more money is taken out of the spending cycle.

    $$MPT = \frac{\text{change in tax}}{\text{change in income}}$$

  - **Marginal Propensity to Import (MPM):** proportion of extra income spent on imported goods. Higher MPM lowers multiplier because spending leaks out of the domestic economy.

    $$MPM = \frac{\text{change in imports}}{\text{change in income}}$$

  - **Marginal Propensity to Withdraw (MPW):** total proportion of extra income withdrawn from the economy through saving, taxes, and imports. The higher the total withdrawals (MPW), the smaller the multiplier. Injections into the economy have less impact on overall GDP growth.

    $$MPW = MPS + MPT + MPM$$

    $$\text{Multiplier} = \frac{1}{MPW}$$

- **Significance of the multiplier for shifts in AD:**
  - When there is a change in injections (investment, government spending or exports) or leakages (savings, taxes or imports), the total effect on the economy is much bigger than the initial change.
  - The larger the multiplier, the greater the impact of any change in injections or withdrawals. This means even a small increase in injections can lead to a much bigger increase in overall economic output. Therefore, the bigger the multiplier, the larger the overall shift in AD.

Causes of economic growth

Economic growth happens when **Long-Run Aggregate Supply (LRAS)** or **Aggregate Demand (AD)** increases. This means the economy's new equilibrium output is higher.

Increase in LRAS	Increase in AD
New technology	Increase in government expenditure
Increase in net migration	Increase in consumption
Increase in investment	Increase in investment

- **Actual vs. potential growth:** actual growth is real increase in GDP (what the economy produces), while potential growth: how much the economy *could* produce if all resources (labour, machinery etc.) were fully employed.
- **Importance of international trade:** when a country exports more goods and services, it leads to an increase in AD (rightward shift). More spending in the economy can lead to higher output and employment.
- **Export led growth:** improves current account on the balance of payments because the country is earning more money from selling goods abroad.

Trade (business) cycle

Economic growth is not steady. It goes through ups and downs over time.
- **Boom:** period of rapid economic growth.
- **Slump:** period of very slow or negative growth.
- **Recession:** when the economy shrinks for two quarters in a row (negative growth for 6 months).
- **Slowdown:** phase between a boom and a slump where growth slows.
- **Recovery:** phase between a slump and a boom where growth starts picking up again.

Characteristics of a boom	Characteristics of a recession
Low unemployment	Rising unemployment rates
Less underemployment	More underemployment
Rising living standards	Declining living standards
Increasing investment levels	Decreasing investment levels

Economic growth

Output gaps
- **Output gap:** difference between actual growth and potential growth.
- **Actual growth rate vs. long-term trend rate:**
  - **Actual growth rate:** how much real GDP (adjusted for inflation) has grown in a single year.
  - **Long-term trend rate:** average growth rate over a longer period. It gives an idea of the economy's usual performance.
- **Negative output gap:**
  - Occurs when actual economic growth is below potential growth.
  - If the current output is at Y_1, but the potential output is at Y_E, there is a negative output gap of $Y_1 \to Y_E$.
  - If AD increases ($AD_1 \to AD_2$) the economy can move closer to potential output, closing the gap.
- **Positive output gap:**
  - Happens when actual growth is higher than what the economy can sustain in the long term.
  - On a classical LRAS curve, this is shown as a temporary boost in output.
  - Since the LRAS is vertical in the long run, this extra output can't be maintained.
  - The positive output gap disappears.
- **Difficulties measuring the output gap:**
  - Output gaps suggest the economy is not using its resources efficiently.
  - It is hard to measure because we can only observe actual output not potential output.
  - Estimating potential output is difficult because:
    - There may be uncertainty about how much spare capacity exists.
    - Resources may not match the needs of the economy.
    - Some production may be moved abroad (making it look like domestic capacity is lower).

Impact of economic growth
- **Benefits:**
  - **For consumers:**
    - Rising real incomes → people can afford more goods and services → higher standard of living.
    - More income → people can eat better → increased life expectancy.
    - Higher incomes → improved overall happiness and wellbeing.
  - **For firms:**
    - Incomes rise → demand for goods and services grow → higher profits.
    - Shareholders benefit from increased returns on their investments.
  - **For government:**
    - Higher real incomes → more tax revenue.
    - This extra revenue can help reduce income inequality through social programs.
  - **For living standards:**
    - Economic growth can help lift people out of poverty by improving access to resources and opportunities.
- **Costs:**
  - **For consumers:**
    - Rapid growth → inflation rises → goods and services are more expensive.
    - People might have to work longer hours → increased stress → reduced overall wellbeing.
  - **For firms:**
    - Higher demand for workers and raw materials → wages increase and input prices rise.
    - Increased costs can reduce profits.
  - **For government:**
    - People earn more → import more → reduced exports → worse trade balance.
  - **For living standards:**
    - Faster growth → sacrificing current consumption → invest in the future.
    - In the long run, living standards improve as the economy's PPF shifts outward.

Macroeconomic objectives and policies

Demand-side policies

Monetary policy instruments: changing monetary variables to affect AD.
- **Interest rates:** cost of borrowing money or the reward for saving.
  - **Interest rates to reduce AD:** if inflation is above the target, the Bank of England's Monetary Policy Committee (MPC) may increase the base interest rate. This makes borrowing more expensive and saving more attractive. This means C falls, I falls, (X – M) may fall as the pound strengthens, and AD decreases → AD curve shifts left, ultimately causing lower inflation and reduced economic growth.
  - **Interest rates to increase AD:** if inflation is below the target, the MPC may lower rates to makes borrowing cheaper and saving less attractive. This means C rises, I rises, (X – M) may rise as the pound weakens, and AD increases → AD curve shifts right, hence an increase in the price level and higher real output. This can be compounded by multiplier effects.
- **Quantitative Easing (QE):** increases money supply in the economy by the Central Bank creating new money and using it to buy government bonds.
  - The Bank of England agrees to buy government bonds/other securities.
  - Commercial banks get cash for their bonds → increasing liquidity.
  - Banks lower their lending rates because they have more cash.
  - Consumers and firms borrow more due to cheaper loans.
  - Increased borrowing boosts consumption and investment.
  - AD rises → causing inflation to increase.
- **Fiscal policy instruments:** use government spending and taxation.
  - **Fiscal policy to reduce AD:**
    - Reduce government spending.
    - Increase taxes.
    - Causes contractionary effect on AD.
    - AD curve shifts left.
    - Multiplier effects can make the impact bigger.
  - **Fiscal policy to increase AD:**
    - Increase government spending.
    - Decrease taxes.
    - Causes an expansionary effect on AD.
    - AD curve shifts right.
    - Multiplier effects can make the rise in output and inflation stronger.

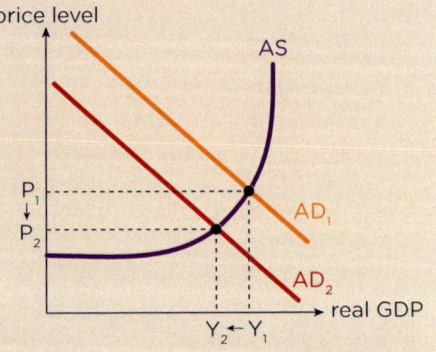

Macroeconomic objectives

- **Economic growth:** sustained increase in the output of goods and services in an economy over time.
- **Low unemployment:** ensuring most people who are willing and able to work can find employment.
- **Low and stable rate of inflation:** maintaining price stability to preserve the purchasing power of money.
- **Balance of payments equilibrium on current account:** achieving a sustainable level of imports and exports without persistent deficits or surpluses.
- **Balanced government budget:** ensuring government spending does not consistently exceed revenue.
- **Protection of the environment:** promoting sustainable use of natural resources and reducing ecological damage.
- **Greater income equality:** reducing disparities in income distribution to promote social fairness and cohesion.

Government budget: deficit and surplus

The government budget can be:
- **Balanced budget:** government revenue = government expenditure
- **Budget deficit:** government revenue < government expenditure
- **Budget surplus:** government revenue > government expenditure

When there is a budget deficit, the government borrows money to cover the gap. This borrowing adds to the public debt.

Direct and indirect taxation

Taxation is the government's main source of revenue. There are two types of taxes:
- **Direct taxes:** charged directly to individuals or firms based on their income or profits. These are paid straight to the government by the person or company (e.g. Income tax, corporation tax).
- **Indirect taxes:** charged on spending (when you buy goods or services). Business selling the goods or services send this tax to the government. The less a consumer spends, the less indirect tax they pay (e.g. VAT).

Macroeconomic objectives and policies

The role of the Bank of England
- **Monetary Policy Committee (MPC)** set the **Bank Rate (main interest rate)** and decide whether to use or continue **quantitative easing (QE)**.
- Their top priority is to keep inflation close to the 2% CPI target.

Strengths of monetary policy	Weaknesses of monetary policy
Bank of England acts independently from the government so decisions are less political and can focus on the economy	Goals can clash (e.g. wanting economic growth but also controlling inflation, which tends to rise with growth)
Can focus on the long-term health of the economy	Long time lags (up to 2 years) before policy effects fully kick in

Strengths of fiscal policy	Weaknesses of fiscal policy
Works faster than monetary policy because spending impacts are more immediate	More government spending can lead to budget deficits creating debt
Can redistribute income fairly through taxes (helping to reduce inequality)	Objectives clash e.g. cutting taxes to increase growth might cause inflation

Below is a table showing demand side fiscal and monetary policy responses in the UK and US to the 2008 global financial crisis.

	Fiscal policy	Monetary policy
UK	• Significant Keynesian fiscal stimulus. • Banks supported and bailed out. • Income tax cuts, VAT reduction, small business loan guarantees introduced. • Switched to austerity policies, cutting government spending and raising taxes (these delayed recovery)	• Bank of England cut Bank Rate from 5.75% to 0.5% in nine cuts. • Multiple rounds of QE worth £375 billion.
USA	• Large Keynesian stimulus to increase AD. • Banks were bailed out to avoid collapse. • Economic Stimulus Act injected $152 billion. • American Recovery and Reinvestment Act injected $787 billion.	• Federal Reserve cut interest rates from 5.25% to 0.25% in eight steps. • Three rounds of QE injected over $3 trillion into the money supply.

Supply-side policies
Supply side policies are used to shift to increase LRAS. This boosts the economy's capacity to produce goods and services sustainably. There are two types of supply side policies:
- **Interventionist supply-side policies:** government steps in directly to fix market failures and boost full employment output.
- **Market-based supply-side policies:** work via the market mechanism.

The impact of supply-side policies can be shown via a rightward shift in the LRAS curve where real GDP/output falls and price level falls.

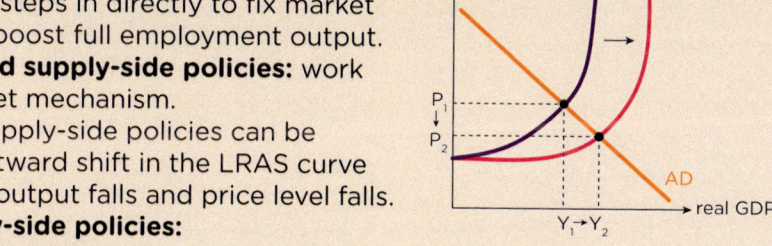

- **Aims of supply-side policies:**
  - **To increase incentives:** for market-based policies, this means cutting income and corporation tax rates (people and businesses want to work and invest more), and restructuring unemployment benefits to encourage job-seeking. For interventionist policies, government programmes can encourage work
  - **To promote competition:** for market-based policies, privatise state-owned firms and deregulate industries, and liberalise trade to boost imports and exports. For interventionist policies, governments spend more on innovation and research through subsidies or direct support to firms to help expand and compete globally.
  - **To reform the labour market:** for market-based policies: reduce trade union power to allow wages to adjust, and lower minimum wages to reduce production costs. For interventionist policies, government investment in programmes to improve occupational mobility (i.e. help workers retrain jobs and move easily between them).
  - **To improve skills and quality of the labour force:** increase government spending on education and retraining programmes, and invest in healthcare to improve worker productivity.
  - **To improve infrastructure:** government boosts spending on transport and infrastructure.

Strengths of supply-side policies	Weaknesses of supply-side policies
Boosts economy long term	Expensive to implement
Helps reduce average price levels	Long-time lags for benefits to occur
Cuts unemployment by making labour market more flexible	Political changes can cause budget cuts or policy reversals

Macroeconomic objectives and policies

Conflicts and trade-offs between policies and objectives
- **Objectives:**
  - **Economic growth vs. inflation:**
    - When the economy grows fast and moves closer to full employment → resources get scarcer.
    - Prices increase (inflation) → go beyond the ideal 2% inflation target.
  - **Economic growth vs. environmental sustainability**
    - Higher growth → more pollution and faster depletion of resources.
    - High growth often hurts the environment.
  - **Economic growth vs. inequality**
    - Owners of capital during periods of economic growth often make more money than workers do.
    - Income inequality worsens.
  - **Economic growth vs. current account balance**
    - When people earn more → import more.
    - Current account (exports minus imports) worsens.
  - **Low unemployment vs. low inflation**
    - Low unemployment → workers become scarce → wages increase.
    - Higher wages → inflation rises → hard to keep prices stable.
- **Policies:**
  - **Contractionary monetary policy:** helps to reduce demand-side inflation, but increases the cost of borrowing for firms and reduces investment (which slows long-term supply-side growth)
  - **Expansionary fiscal policy:** helps boost long-term growth by improving LRAS, but in the short run can cause excess demand → leads to inflation.
- **Short-Run Phillips Curve (SRPC):** shows short-run trade-off between inflation and unemployment.
  - Rising inflation is linked to falling unemployment.
  - Rising unemployment is linked to falling inflation.
  - Due to this, governments often struggle to achieve both low unemployment and low inflation at the same time.

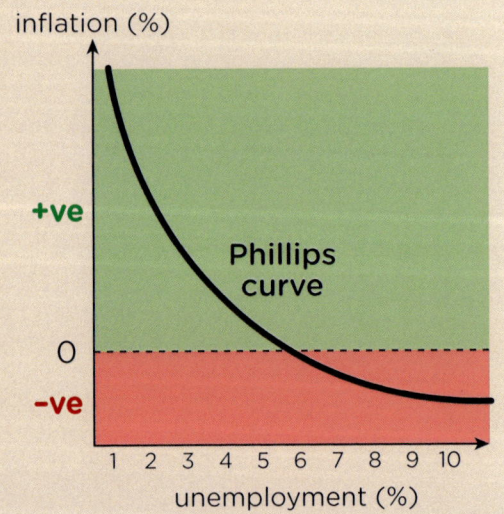

Sizes and types of firms

All specs except: AQA

- **Why some firms remain small**
  - **Size of the market is small:** not enough demand to justify expansion.
  - **Personalised services:** firms like nail bars rely on personal connections with customers.
  - **Limited access to finance:** small firms are often seen as risky by banks, making it harder to get loans.
- **Why some firms grow:**
  - **Benefit from economies of scale:** larger firms have lower long-run average costs
  - **Increase their market share:** gives firms more power to set prices and reduces competitive threats
  - **Reduce risk:** diversification allows firms to spread risk across different products (economies of scope).
- **Principal-agent problem:**
  - Shareholders (principals) own large firms but hire managers (agents) to run them.
  - Shareholders want to maximise profits, but managers might prioritise sales or other goals
  - Conflict arises when the interests of the principals and agents diverge.
- **Public vs. private sector firms:**
  - Public sector firms are owned by the government and don't need to make a profit as losses can be covered by taxation (e.g. policing, education, healthcare). Some public sector firms (e.g. Network Rail) may aim to make a profit but often prioritise service quality.
  - Private sector firms are owned by private individuals or groups and aim to make a profit to survive (e.g. sole proprietors, partnerships).
- **Profit vs. not-for-profit organisations:**
  - Profit organisations aim to make or maximise profit.
  - Not-for-profit organisations operate in the private sector but don't aim to make private profit for directors, members, or shareholders (e.g. charities), instead reinvesting any surplus back into the organisation.

Business growth

Business growth

All specs except: AQA

- **Methods of business growth:**
  - **Organic growth:** internal growth using the firm's own resources. This is achieved through buying new capital, hiring more staff, and increasing working hours.

Advantages	Disadvantages
Managers already know the business well	May reduce competitiveness
Firm can adapt quickly to market changes	Firm may become too specialised in areas that are becoming outdated
Less risky than mergers	Growth may be slower than with mergers

  - **Vertical integration:** when a business joins with another at a different stage of the production chain, as shown on the right.
  - **Forward vertical integration:** if a firm merges with one later in the chain (closer to the final customers)

producers → suppliers → manufacturers → retailers → customers (backwards / forwards)

Advantages	Disadvantages
Helps reduce distractions from competing products, giving the business more control	Business might not offer a big enough range to attract customers on its own
Easier to gather feedback from customers and adjust products quickly	If the end product doesn't sell, losses can be bigger since the firm controls more stages

  - **Backward vertical integration:** if a firm merges with one earlier in the chain (further from the final customer)

Advantages	Disadvantages
More control over materials, prices, and quality	Firm may not need all the supplies it is producing
Profit made by the supplier now goes straight to the business	Might lack expertise in that part of the chain, leading to higher costs

  - **Horizontal integration:** when two businesses at the **same stage** of the same production process join. They may not make identical products but want to expand the variety they offer, thus this can be a way to enter new international markets.

Advantages	Disadvantages
Cuts costs through economies of scale	Business may rely too much on a limited number of products or services
Lowers risk of being taken over by competitors	Job losses may happen if both firms had people doing the same roles

  - **Conglomerate integration:** when a business takes over or merges with another in a totally different industry.

Advantages	Disadvantages
Increases brand awareness and reputation across different markets	Firm may not understand the new industry well, leading to mistakes.
Spreads risk (strong profits in one part of the business can help cover losses in another)	Differences in how the two businesses operate could lead to clashes and lower efficiency

- **Constraints on business growth** include **market size** (e.g. in small/niche markets with low demand, there's limited potential to expand), **access to finance** (smaller firms often struggle to secure loans), **owner objectives** (preferring to keep full control or avoid complications), and **government regulation** (can protect competition and stop monopolies).

Demergers

All specs except: AQA

Demergers are when a business splits into two or more separate firms. This can be to **boost profits** (selling off unprofitable parts of the business), to **raise money** (selling shares to obtain capital to invest), or **due to regulatory pressure** (if forced to split up to reduce market dominance and boost competition). The impacts of demergers:

- **On businesses:** can focus more on core operations, freeing up funds for investment or getting rid of parts that are dragging profits down.
- **On workers:** job security may improve if weak divisions are removed, and there is less internal conflict between different areas of the business.
- **On consumers:** more competition can lead to lower prices, and smaller firms may better meet consumer needs, though some services or products might become harder to access if the firm specialises.

Business objectives

Business objectives

All specs except: AQA

- **Profit maximisation:** when a firm aims to earn the highest possible profit. There are two key ways to define profit maximisation:
  - When the difference between total revenue (TR) and total cost (TC) is at its maximum.
  - When marginal revenue (MR) = marginal cost (MC) (the revenue gained from selling one more unit is exactly equal to the cost of producing that unit).
- **Revenue maximisation:** when a firm aims to generate the highest total revenue, regardless of profit. It happens when either:
  - Total revenue (TR) is at its maximum.
  - Marginal revenue (MR) = 0 (selling one more unit adds nothing to total revenue).
  - **Reason for revenue maximisation:**
    - The firm needs to clear all stock, so cost doesn't matter.
    - If there is separation between ownership and control, managers might pursue sales while owners care about profit.
    - If a takeover is likely, the firm may push up revenues to increase its valuation.
- **Sales maximisation:** when a firm aims to sell as much as possible while covering its costs (earning normal profit). It occurs when either:
  - Total revenue = total cost (TR = TC).
  - Average revenue = average cost (AR = AC).
  - **Reasons for sale maximisation:**
    - To increase market share or deter new entrants (low prices and high sales can scare off potential rivals).
    - To avoid attention from competition regulators.
- **Satisficing:** when firms aim for an acceptable level of multiple objectives, rather than maximising one. Profit satisficing is earning sufficient (not maximum) profit. **Reasons for satisficing** include when there is a divide between owners/shareholders and managers/directors, or the only aim is to make just enough profit to keep shareholders happy while also focusing on other goals (growth, staff wellbeing etc.).

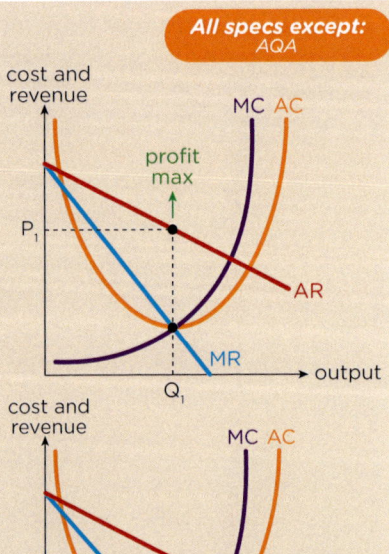

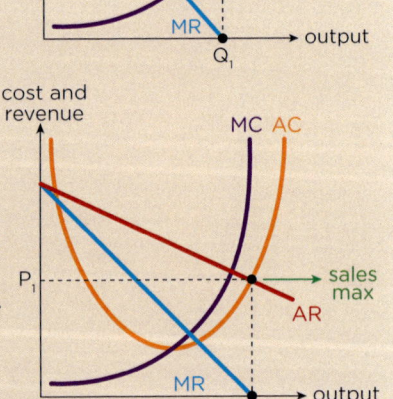

Revenue

- If a firm is operating in a perfectly competitive market, it is a **price taker,** meaning the firm must accept the market-determined price.
- If a firm is operating in an imperfectly competitive market, it is a **price maker,** meaning the firm can influence the price.
- Formulas for revenue concepts:
  - **Total Revenue (TR):** total income a firm gets from selling a certain quantity of goods or services at a set price.

    TR = Price (P) × Quantity (Q)
  - **Average Revenue (AR):** revenue earned per unit sold.

    AR = TR ÷ Q
  - **Marginal Revenue (MR):** extra revenue a firm gets from selling one additional unit.

    MR = Change in TR ÷ Change in Q

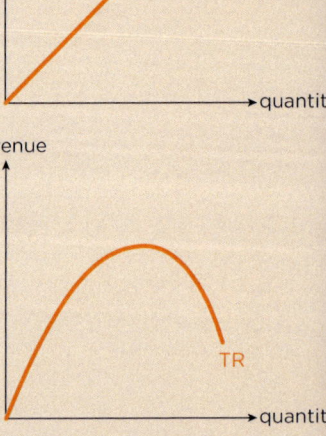

- PED and revenue concepts:
  - **Price Elasticity of Demand (PED)** measures how responsive the quantity demanded is to changes in price. The formula is:

    PED = Change in quantity demanded ÷ Change in price
  - **Elastic demand (PED > 1):** when demand is elastic, even a small price change causes a bigger change in quantity demanded.
    - If the firm lowers price, total revenue goes up because more units are sold.
    - If the firm increases price, total revenue goes down as demand falls by more.
  - **Unitary elastic demand (PED = 1):**
    - A price change causes the same percentage change in quantity demanded.
    - Total revenue stays unchanged regardless of price increases or decreases.
  - **Inelastic demand (PED < 1):**
    - Demand doesn't change much with price.
    - If the firm lowers price, total revenue goes down.
    - If the firm raises price, total revenue goes up because the drop in demand is small.

Revenue, costs, and profits

Costs
- **Formulas for cost concepts:**
  - **Total Cost (TC)** = Total Fixed Cost (TFC) + Total Variable Cost (TVC)
    - **Total Fixed Cost (TFC):** stays constant regardless of output level.
    - **Total Variable Cost (TVC):** changes with production (more output = higher TVC).
  - **Average Total Cost (ATC)** = TC ÷ Quantity of Output
    - **Average Fixed Cost (AFC):** AFC = TFC ÷ Quantity of Output
    - **Average Variable Cost (AVC):** AVC = TVC ÷ Quantity of Output
  - **Marginal Cost (MC):** shows the extra cost of producing one more unit.
    MC = Change in Total Cost (ΔTC) ÷ Change in Quantity (ΔQ)
    - If **MC < ATC**, then ATC is falling.
    - If **MC > ATC**, then ATC is rising.
    - If **MC = ATC**, then ATC is at its minimum
- **Relationship between SRAC and LRAC curves:**
  - In the short run, some inputs are fixed (e.g. factory size), so firms can only adjust variable inputs. In the long run, all inputs are variable.
  - The LRAC curve (long-run average cost) shows the lowest possible average cost a firm can achieve at any output level.
  - The LRAC touches each SRAC at the point where that SRAC is most efficient. LRACs are usually flatter than SRACs.

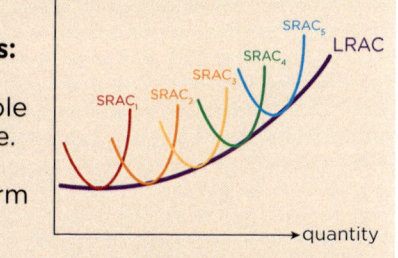

Normal profits, supernormal profits, and losses
- **Normal profit:** minimum profit needed to keep the firm running; covers all costs including opportunity costs (TR = TC).
- **Supernormal profit:** occurs when total revenue is greater than total cost (TR > TC). Firm earns extra profit, attracting competition until profits fall.
- **Losses:** when total cost exceeds total revenue (TC > TR).
- **Break-even point:** AR=AC and TR=TC, when no supernormal profit or losses are made.
- **Shutdown points:**
  - **Short-run shutdown:** if total revenue is less than variable costs (TR < VC), firm should stop producing to avoid bigger losses since the fixed costs still apply.
  - **Long-run shutdown:** if total revenue is less than total costs (TR < TC), firm should exit the industry because it can't cover all expenses.

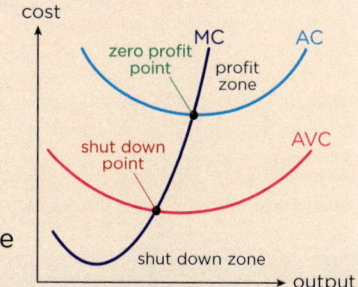

Economies and diseconomies of scale
- **Types of economies of scale:**
  - **Technical economies:** when a company grows bigger and more efficient.
  - **Managerial economies:** bigger companies often have expert managers who focus on specific areas.
  - **Marketing economies:** large firms can spend more on advertising and marketing so cost per product goes down and they get more customers.
  - **Financial economies:** big companies get better loan deals with lower interest rates and can negotiate better prices from suppliers.
  - **Risk-bearing economies:** large firms can handle sudden changes in the market better which lowers costs.
- **Types of diseconomies of scale:**
  - **Managerial diseconomies:** when companies get too big, their management can be confusing and slow, making things less efficient.
  - **Coordination and control problems:** harder for large companies to keep all departments working smoothly together, which can raise costs.
  - **Worker alienation:** employees in big companies may feel less connected to the business, causing lower motivation and more people quitting.
  - **Communication challenges:** as a company grows, it becomes tough to communicate well, leading to mistakes and higher costs.
- **Minimum Efficient Scale (MES):** the smallest amount of production where a company gets the lowest average cost per unit. Producing more beyond this point can make costs rise due to diseconomies of scale.
  - Companies working at or near MES can compete because costs are low.
  - MES differs between industries and depends on technology, demand, and how products are made.
  - Companies producing less than MES have higher costs and struggle to compete, while those producing too much may face inefficiencies.
- **Distinction between internal and external economies of scale:**
  - **Internal economies of scale:**
    - Cost savings that come from inside the company as it grows.
    - They happen because company improves its processes, workers specialise, and management gets better.
    - Only the company itself controls these savings.
  - **External economies of scale:**
    - Cost benefits happen when many companies in the same industry or area grow together. They come from things like more skilled workers nearby, better suppliers, improved infrastructure, or support from the local business environment.
    - No single company controls these, all firms in the area benefit.

Market structures

Efficiency
- **Allocative efficiency:** resources are used to maximise overall welfare. Achieved when price equals marginal cost (P = MC), meaning the right amount of goods are produced to satisfy consumers.
- **Productive efficiency:** producing goods at the lowest cost possible. Happens when firms operate at the minimum point of the average cost curve (AC = MC), avoiding waste.
- **Dynamic efficiency:** economy's ability to innovate and improve over time with technology and adapting to changes, supporting long-term growth.
- **X-inefficiency:** occurs when firms fail to minimise costs despite little competition, often due to poor management or lack of motivation. Common in firms with market power.
- **Efficiency in market structures:**
  - **Perfect competition:** achieves both allocative and productive efficiency, firms are price takers producing at lowest costs.
  - **Monopoly:** usually, allocatively inefficient since prices are above marginal cost, causing deadweight loss but can be productively efficient if costs are minimised.
  - **Monopolistic competition:** allocative and productive efficiency are not fully reached because firms have some market power and don't produce at minimum average cost due to product differentiation.
  - **Oligopoly:** may lack allocative efficiency but often invest in R&D, enhancing dynamic efficiency. Productive efficiency varies by industry.
  - **Mixed/regulated markets:** government intervention aims to improve efficiency via regulations, subsidies, or antitrust actions.

Perfect competition
- **Characteristics of perfect competition:**
  - **Large number of sellers:** no single firm can influence the market price.
  - **Homogeneous products:** firms sell identical goods/perfect substitutes.
  - **Perfect information:** buyers and sellers have full knowledge of goods/services (symmetric information).
  - **Free entry and exit:** firms can enter or leave the market without barriers, keeping competition high (low sunk costs).
  - **Price takers:** firms accept market price and adjust output accordingly, they have no pricing power.
  - **Zero economic profit in the long run:** in the long run, firms only make normal profit (enough to cover their costs).
  - **Perfect resource mobility:** labour/capital moves freely between firms.
  - **Non-collusive behaviour:** firms compete independently and don't cooperate to influence prices.

- **Profit-maximising equilibrium:**
  - **Short run:**
    - A firm maximises profit where MC = P.
    - If MC < P, firms should increase output.
    - If MC > P, firms should decrease output.
    - The firm keeps producing as long as P is greater than or equal to AVC, even if it is making a loss (as long as fixed costs are being covered).

  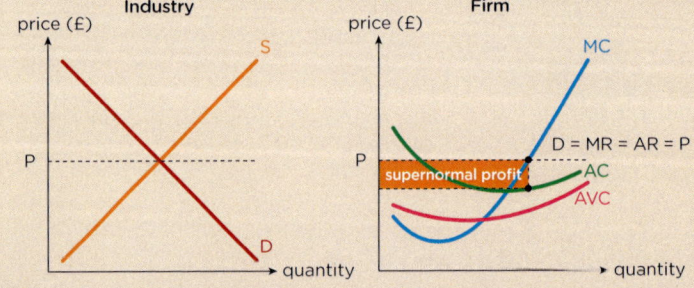

  - **Long run:**
    - If firms are making supernormal profits, new firms enter the market, raising supply and lowering price, until P = ATC.
    - If firms face losses, some firms exit the market, meaning supply falls and price rises until the remaining firms return to normal profit.
    - Long-run equilibrium occurs when P = MC = ATC (firms earn normal profit and there is no incentive exists to enter or exit).

  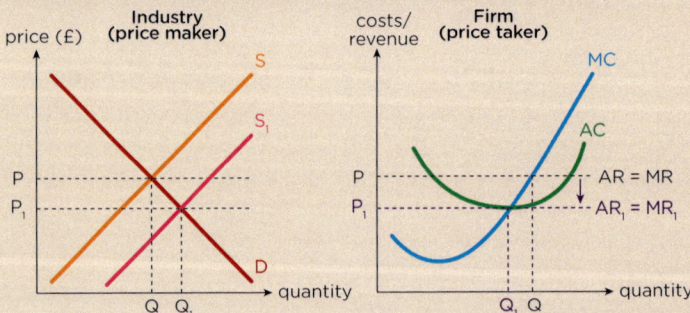

  - Left diagram: entry of new firms into industry means market supply curve shifts to right. This results in an increase in market supply (Q to Q_1) and fall in prices (P to P_1).
  - Right diagram: individual firms face lower price (P to P_1 and lower output (Q to Q_1). At lower prices, firms want to operate at slightly lower output (MR is lower). This decrease in market prices means firms will only make normal profit (AR=AC).

Market structures

Monopolistic competition
- **Characteristics of monopolistically competitive markets:**
  - **Many sellers:** numerous firms operate.
  - **Product differentiation:** products are similar but not identical.
  - **Easy entry and exit:** firms can freely enter or leave the market due to low barriers like minimal start-up costs or regulation.
  - **Non-price competition:** firms compete through advertising, branding and product innovation rather than solely on price.
  - **Limited price control:** due to differentiation, firms have some power over pricing but competition limits how much they can raise prices without losing customers.
  - **Short-run and long-run profits:** economic profits or losses can occur in the short run. In the long run, new entrants or changing strategies usually drive profits to zero.
  - **Imperfect information:** consumers don't always have complete knowledge of all products, making branding and advertising effective tools for firms.
- **Profit maximising equilibrium:**
  - **Short run:**
    - Monopolistically competitive firm maximises profit where MC = MR.
    - From this output level, firm charges price found on demand curve.
    - If P > ATC, economic profit is earned.
    - If ATC > P > AVC, the firm makes a loss but still produces to cover variable costs.
    - If P < AVC, the firm shuts down temporarily.

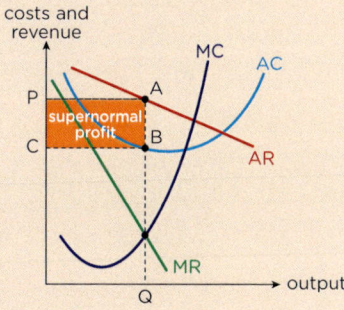

  - **Long run:**
    - If economic profits exist, new firms enter market due to low entry barriers.
    - Increased competition shifts each firm's demand curve leftwards (due to more substitutes), reducing its market share.
    - Over time, economic profits fall to zero and firms only make normal profit (P=ATC).
    - If firms face losses, some will exit the market, resulting in less competition and a rightward shift in the demand for remaining firms.
    - Long-run equilibrium is reached when firms cover all costs but make zero economic profit.

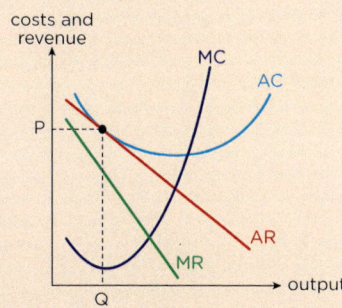

Oligopoly
- **Characteristics of oligopoly:**
  - **High barriers to entry and exit:** starting/leaving the market is difficult.
  - **High concentration ratio:** small number of firms control most of the market, meaning the actions of one firm can affect the whole industry.
  - **Interdependence of firms:** businesses don't make decisions in isolation. If one changes price or releases something new, the others react quickly.
  - **Products differentiation:** even if the products are similar, firms try to stand out using branding/packaging to attract customers.
- **N-firm concentration ratio:** total market share (%) of the top 'n' firms.
  - This tells us how concentrated the market is – a high ratio means fewer firms control the market, so there is less competition. This is used by regulators to spot when an industry might be too dominated or unfair.
- **Reasons for collusive and non-collusive behaviour:**
  - **Collusive reasons** (e.g. wanting to keep prices high and avoid losing profits, avoids undercutting, and less competition means more stability).
  - **Non-collusive reasons** (e.g. wanting to outdo each other and gain market share, or pursues different goals and priorities).
- **Collusion types, cartels, and price leadership:**
  - **Overt collusion:** openly working together and direct contract is involved (where firms agree on things like price or supply)
  - **Tacit collusion:** silent understanding; everyone follows the market leader.
  - **Cartels:** agreement between big firms to fix prices or limit supply (illegal in most places).
  - **Price leadership:** when one dominant firm sets a price and everyone else copies without discussing it.
- **Prisoner's dilemma with two firms:** if two rival firms agree to charge high prices and both stick to it, there will be high profits for both. However, if one breaks the deal and lowers their price, they will likely get more customers. If the other firm then drops prices, they're both worse off.
- **Types of price competition:**
  - **Price war:** constantly lower prices to beat rivals (hurts profit margins).
  - **Predatory pricing:** one firm cuts prices super low to force others out then raises them again once they're other firms have exited the market.
  - **Limit pricing:** charging just low enough to stop new firms entering.
- **Types of non-price competition:**
  - **Making your product stand out:** improving quality, features or branding
  - **Advertising:** helps to awareness and loyalty
  - **Innovation:** releasing new versions to keep ahead of the game.
  - **Service:** customers get perks (e.g. support, warranties, customisation).
  - **Distribution:** making your product easier to buy by being in more stores or online platforms.

Market structures

Monopoly
- **Characteristics of monopoly:**
  - **Sole provider:** only one firm supplies the product; no alternatives.
  - **No substitutes:** the good or service sold has no close replacements, giving the firm control over pricing.
  - **Entry is difficult:** other firms can't easily join the market due to things like patents, huge start-up costs or legal restrictions.
  - **Sets its own price:** since there's no competition, the monopolist decides how much to charge and how much to produce.
- **Profit maximising equilibrium:** a monopoly earns the most when it produces at the point where MR = MC. Working out the MC curve shows how much it costs to produce extra units.

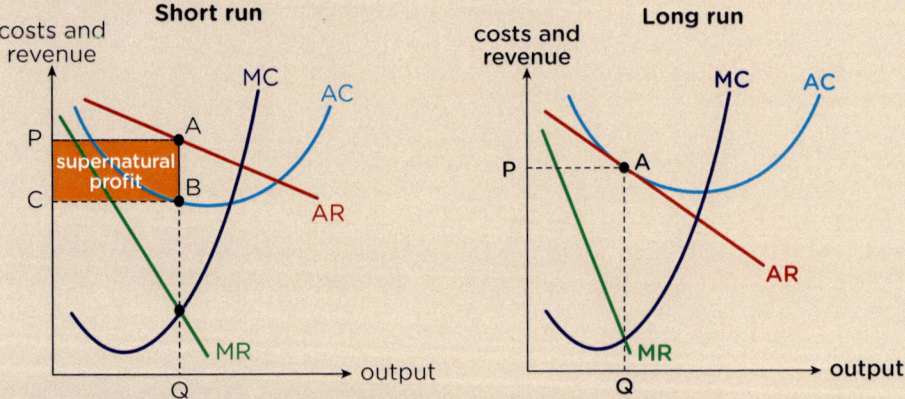

- **Third degree price discrimination:**
  - **Groups must be separable:** the firm needs to split consumers by location, age, or another trait.
  - **Different sensitivities to price:** some groups are more willing to pay.
  - **No reselling:** customers can't buy at the lower price and sell for profit.
  - **Costs and benefits:** producers get higher profits by charging more strategically, and some consumers get a better deal but others lose out.

- **Advantages and disadvantages of monopolies:**
  - **For the firm:** long-term profit and control, but also the risk of regulators stepping in.
  - **For buyers:** higher prices and limited choice.
  - **For workers:** jobs can be stable, but wages may suffer due to lack of competition.
  - **For suppliers:** low price due to the monopoly's power.
- **Natural monopoly:** some markets are best served by just one firm. The characteristics of a natural monopoly are: high fixed costs compared to running costs; the more they produce, the cheaper it gets per unit; and having more than one supplier would be wasteful or unrealistic due to infrastructure costs.
- **Price discrimination graphs:**

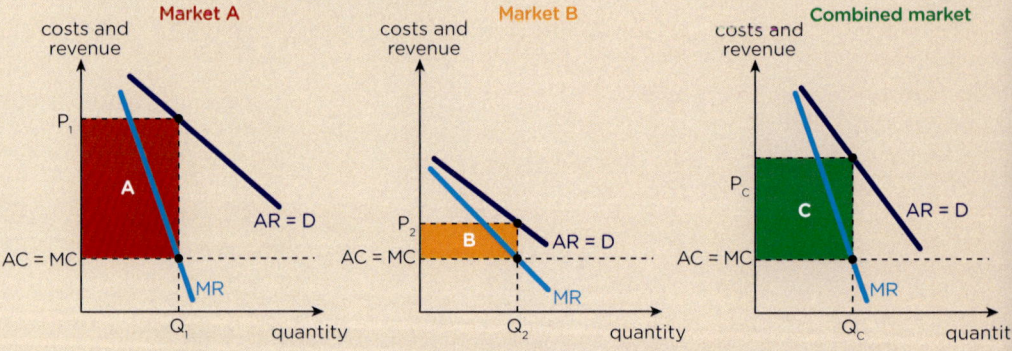

- Market A (inelastic demand) and Market B (elastic demand) and the combined market.
- AC is constant (AC=MC curve is horizontal line).
- In the combined market, MC=MR to maximise price (P_c) with output (Q_c) and profit = C.
- In Market A: profit maximising output is Q_1 and price P_1.
- Market B: profit maximising output is Q_2 and price P_2.
- Price is higher in Market A (inelastic demand) than Market B (elastic demand).
- Total profit for Market A is area A and total profit for Market B is area B.
- Price discrimination results in increase in supernormal profit (area A + area B greater than area C).

Market structures

Monopsony

A monopsony is a firm that is the sole buyer of resources or supplies.
- **Characteristics and conditions of a monopsony:**
  - **One main buyer:** one firm or organisation does most of the buying. They have major control over how much is bought and at what price.
  - **Few alternatives for sellers:** since sellers have limited other buyers to sell to, they are less able to negotiate better deals.
  - **Buyer sets the price:** since sellers can't easily go elsewhere, the monopsonist can push prices down (they decide how much they're willing to pay)
- **Costs and benefits of a monopsony:**
  - For the monopsonist:
    - Benefit: they can cut costs by negotiating lower prices for resources, raw materials, or labour.
    - Cost: if they push prices too low, suppliers could struggle, leading to shortages, lower quality, or firms dropping out.
  - For consumers:
    - Benefit: lower production costs may mean cheaper prices for goods.
    - Cost: if suppliers reduce quality or stop selling, the variety and quality of products can suffer in the long term.
  - For employees:
    - Benefit: some large buyers might offer job security, regular hours and benefits.
    - Cost: if they use their power to keep wages down, workers might earn less than they would in a competitive market. It can also limit job choices.
  - For suppliers:
    - Benefit: monopsonist can provide a stable and consistent source of demand.
    - Cost: power imbalance can mean suppliers are forced to accept low prices, reduced profits, and a weakened bargaining position.

Contestability

- **Characteristics of contestable markets:**
  - **Low barriers to entry:** easy for new firms to enter (low start up costs and light regulation)
  - **Low barriers to exit:** firms can leave market without big financial losses.
  - **Perfect information:** all firms have full access to information on prices, costs, and demand (no firm has an information advantage).
  - **No sunk costs:** sunk costs are money you can't get back. In contestable markets, sunk costs are assumed to be very low or non-existent.
  - **Freedom to enter and exit:** firms can enter or exit out of the market freely (no legal restrictions or licensing delays).
  - **No collusion:** firms don't collude because they know by increasing prices, new competitors will be attracted who will undercut them.
- **Implications of contestable markets for behaviour of firms:**
  - **Strong price competition:** firms keep prices low to prevent new entrants from stealing customers. Charging too much = competition.
  - **Focus on efficiency and innovation:** to stay ahead of possible new competitors, firms try to operate more efficiently and improve their products.
  - **Short-term profit focus:** market conditions can shift fast, firms tend to focus more on short-term gains rather than long-term dominance.
  - **No lasting monopoly power:** big firms can't hold onto market power for long, since anyone could come in and compete effectively if conditions are favourable.
- **Types of barriers to entry and exit:**
  - **Economies of scale:** big firms can produce at lower costs, making it hard for smaller newcomers to compete.
  - **Capital requirements:** some industries require big upfront investment which can be expensive for new firms.
  - **Government regulation:** licensing, permit or rules can delay or block new entrants.
  - **Brand loyalty:** well-known brands make it harder for new businesses to attract customers.
- **Sunk costs and degree of contestability:**
  - **Low sunk costs = high contestability:** if firms don't risk losing money when leaving a market, they are more likely to enter in the first place, keeping markets competitive.
  - **High sunk costs = low contestability:** if firms have sunk a lot of money into things they can't recover, they are less likely to leave (even if they're not making profits), reducing how contestable the market is.

Labour market

Demand and supply of labour
- Demand for labour is derived (i.e. depends on) demand.
- Factors that influence demand for labour include:
  - **Price of the final product:** higher product price → higher marginal revenue product (MRP) → more labour demanded.
  - **Demand for the final product:** booming economy → increased demand for goods/services → increased labour demand.
  - **Substitution of capital:** if machines are cheaper/more efficient → labour demand decreases.
  - **Labour productivity:** more productive workers → lower unit costs → increased labour demand.
- Supply depends on how easy it is for workers to enter or stay in a job.
- Factors that influence supply for labour include:
  - **Training period:** long training → lower supply.
  - **Wages in other jobs:** better pay elsewhere → lower supply.
  - **Migration policy:** open borders → more supply.
  - **Income tax levels:** high taxes → less incentive to work → lower supply
  - **Welfare benefits:** high benefits → less incentive to work (especially for low-skilled jobs) → lower supply
- Causes of labour market failure:
  - **Geographical immobility:** can't move due to family, housing, transport, etc.
  - **Occupational immobility:** can't switch jobs due to lack of transferable skills, leading to structural unemployment.

Wage determination in competitive/non-competitive markets
- **Labour market equilibrium:**
  - Demand for Labour (DL) = Supply of Labour (SL) where firms are demanders and workers are suppliers.
  - If wage is too low → hard to recruit
  - If wage is too high → too many applicants
  - Equilibrium at DL = SL at W_e and Q_e.
  - At equilibrium there is no excess supply and no excess demand.
- **Current labour market issues:**
  - Skills shortages: in key areas like healthcare and digital technology.
  - Youth unemployment: due to lack of experience or skills mismatch.
  - Raising retirement ages: more pensioners and longer life expectancy.
  - Zero-hour contracts: no guaranteed hours or benefits, distorting unemployment data.

Labour market interventions
- **Minimum wages**
  - Set above market equilibrium (W_e).
  - Supply increases from $Q_e → Q_s$.
  - Demand falls from $Q_e → Q_d$.
  - There is excess supply, so unemployment is given by $Q_s - Q_d$.
  - Advantages: prevents exploitation and can help reduce poverty.
  - Disadvantages: causes unemployment and could be inflationary if firms decide to pass on higher costs to consumers.
- **Maximum wage:**
  - Set below market equilibrium (W_e).
  - Supply decreases from $Q_e → Q_s$.
  - Demand increases from $Q_e → Q_d$.
  - There is excess demand (worker shortage).
  - Advantages: can reduce income inequality and allows higher wages to be earned by more workers.
  - Disadvantages: leads to worker shortage and reduces incentives to work certain jobs.
- **Public sector wage setting**
  - The government is the biggest employer and can act as a monopsony (sole buyer of labour)
  - Changes in public sector pay impact taxpayer burden and worker strikes
- **Policies to tackle labour market immobility:**
  - **Education/training:** skilled workers → easier job switching → reduces occupational immobility
  - **Targeting shortages:** provide training for in demand jobs
  - **Relocation subsidies:** help people move to where jobs are → reduces geographical immobility.
- **Elasticity of labour:**
  - **Elasticity of demand for labour (PED):** measures how much a firm's demand for labour changes when wage rate changes.
    - If PED is elastic, then there will be a larger fall in demand.
    - If PED is inelastic, then there will be a smaller fall in demand.
  - **Elasticity of supply of labour (PES):** measures how much a firm's labour supplied changes when wage rate changes.
    - If PES is elastic, then there will be a larger rise in supply.
    - If PES is inelastic, then there will be a smaller rise in supply.

Government intervention and globalisation

Government interventions

- **Government intervention to control mergers:**
  - Competition and Markets Authority (CMA) investigates mergers if one firm has turnover of £70m+, or their combined market share is equal to 25%+. The CMA force demergers if they deem them inappropriate.
- **Government intervention to control monopolies**
  - **Price regulation:** government regulates price in several industries (e.g. OFGEM: price cap on energy, OFWAT: water and sewage, ORR: rail fare regulation).
  - **Profit regulation:** government can set maximum profit as % of assets. However, there is less incentive to invest wisely.
  - **Quality standards:** government can control quality of provision of services by setting quality standards (e.g. care quality commission sets standards for hospitals/care homes)
  - **Performance targets:** businesses can be set specific measurable targets (e.g. rail firms set punctuality targets).
- **Government intervention to promote competition and contestability:**
  - **Support for small businesses:** start-up loans (up to £25,000) and tax reliefs.
  - **Deregulation:** removing barriers to entry to allow more competition.
  - **Competitive tendering:** private firms bid for government contracts (e.g. hospital cleaning) to ensure best value and efficiency.
  - **Privatisation:** state businesses sold to private firms. Leads to efficiency as firms can't rely on subsidies.
- **Government intervention to protect suppliers and employees:**
  - **Restricting monopsony power:** stops big firms from exploiting suppliers (e.g. forcing low prices).
  - **Nationalisation:** state takes over private firms to protect jobs or critical industries.
- **Impact of government intervention:**
  - **On prices:** high competition → low prices → high consumer surplus
  - **On profits:** could decrease if regulation limits pricing power
  - **On efficiency:** high competition → pressure to cut costs
  - **On quality:** more competition → better quality
  - **On choice:** high competition → more options for consumers
- **Limits to government intervention:**
  - **Regulatory capture:** regulators act in favour of firms instead of consumers.
  - **Asymmetric information:** firms know more than regulators so it's hard for them to detect anti-competitive behaviour.

Globalisation

Globalisation refers to increased economic, social, and cultural integration between countries.

- **Characteristics of globalisation:**
  - **Increased trade:** means trade becomes a bigger percentage of GDP.
  - **FDI increases:** more foreign direct investment → global businesses expanding production abroad.
  - **Increased capital flows:** more cross-border mergers and acquisitions.
  - **More movement of people:** labour migration, tourism etc.
- **Factors contributing to globalisation:**
  - **Lower transport costs:** containerisation → economies of scale → reduced LRAC.
  - **Lower communication costs:** internet and technology
  - **Fewer trade barriers:** WTO and international cooperation.
  - **Rise of trading blocs:** EU, NAFTA, etc. encouraging regional trade.
  - **Growth of TNCs:** TNCs offshore to low cost countries and invest via FDI.
  - **Financial market liberalisation:** deregulation and global integration of capital markets → capital flows more freely across borders.
  - **Global supply chains:** advances in logistics and inventory management (e.g., just-in-time production) → economic integration across countries.
  - **Rising incomes and consumer demand:** growth in emerging economies has increased global demand for a wider variety of goods and services, incentivising firms to expand internationally.
  - **Trade liberalisation in developing economies:** countries like China and India opening up their economies since the 1980s–1990s has added billions of consumers and producers to global markets.
- **Impacts of globalisation:**
  - **On countries:** no competitive advantage → more imports → trade deficit risk.
  - **On governments:** increased tax revenue from bigger corporate profits → can spend on services. Some firms can avoid tax using loopholes.
  - **On producers:** can scale up → economies of scale → more profit. Technology transfer from TNCs. Local, uncompetitive firms can be pushed out.
  - **On consumers:** lower prices → higher consumer surplus, and more variety in goods/services.
  - **On workers:** more jobs in some areas, though there is a risk of exploitation in developing countries (low wages, long hours).
  - **On environment:** more transport → air and noise pollution, and resource depletion as raw materials are over-extracted.

International economics

Specialisation and trade

- **Absolute advantage:** country has absolute advantage when it can produce more using fewer inputs than another country. For example, the graph on the right shows Country A has absolute advantage in Good X, and Country B has absolute advantage in Good Y.
- **Comparative advantage:** country has comparative advantage when it can produce a good with a lower opportunity cost than another country. This specialisation increases total output. For example, the graph on the right shows Country B has absolute advantage in both goods, but it should produce the one that has the lowest opportunity cost.
  - **Assumptions of comparative advantage:**
    - **No transport costs:** model ignores the cost of moving goods between countries.
    - **Perfect information:** countries are assumed to know where their strengths lie.
    - **Easy factor substitution:** assumed that economies can shift between labour and capital easily.
    - **Constant returns:** theory doesn't consider economies of scale. It assumes production costs stay flat as output increases.
  - **Limitations of comparative advantage:**
    - **Over-dependence:** countries become reliant on imports.
    - **Environmental harm:** resource overuse and pollution from production.
    - **Uneven income distribution:** gains from trade often go to wealthier areas of society.
    - **Structural unemployment:** industries that can't compete may collapse and workers may struggle to retrain jobs or relocate.

- **International specialisation and trade:**

Advantages	Disadvantages
Lower prices: trade leads to cheaper goods and services	**Unemployment:** local industries may not survive global competition, leading to job losses and structural unemployment
More variety: consumers get access to more diverse products	**Trade deficits:** some countries imports are greater than exports so may be weak competitors.
Better quality: competition forces firms to improve products	**Over-specialisation:** developing countries often rely on just one or two exports, leaving them vulnerable to price shocks
Improved living standards: cheaper goods mean more jobs and better services	**Loss of culture:** globalisation can dilute local cultures and traditions

Patterns and terms of trade

Factors that influence **patterns of trade** between countries include:
- Changes in comparative advantage
- Impact of emerging economies
- Growth of trading blocs and bilateral trading agreements
- Changes in relative exchange rates

Terms of trade are a ratio between a country's export and import prices.
- **Factors influencing the terms of trade:**
  - **Relative inflation rates:** if domestic inflation is higher than that of trading partners → terms of trade may worsen.
  - **Comparative productivity:** a country that boosts productivity relative to others may improve its trade terms.
  - **Exchange rate:** stronger currency tends to improve the terms of trade (imports become cheaper).
- **Impacts of changes in terms of trade:**
  - **Rising living standards:** improvement in the terms of trade → country can afford more imports for the same quantity of exports → potentially raising household consumption and living standards.
  - **Current account deterioration:** improved terms of trade seems beneficial → they can reduce export competitiveness → possibly worsening the current account if exports decline as a result.

International economics

Trading blocs and the World Trade Organisation

Trading blocs are alliances between countries aiming to reduce or eliminate trade barriers within the group.

Advantages of trading blocs	Disadvantages of trading blocs
Trade creation: removing internal trade barriers increases trade flow for member countries.	**Trade diversion:** cheaper goods from outside the bloc are replaced by costlier goods from member nations due to external tariffs.
Stronger bargaining power: larger blocs can negotiate more favourable terms in international trade agreements.	**Misallocation of resources:** barriers to non-member countries can disrupt pattern of specialisation based on comparative advantage

Types of trading blocs:
- **Free trade areas:** member nations eliminate tariffs among themselves but maintain independent trade policies for non-members.
- **Customs unions:** free internal trade and members apply a common external tariff to non-members.
- **Common markets:** build on customs unions and allow free movement of goods, services, capital and labour across borders.
- **Monetary unions:** common markets but these adopt a single currency across member countries (e.g. Eurozone).

Advantages of monetary unions	Disadvantages of monetary unions
Reduced transaction costs: no need to exchange currencies within the union, reducing costs	**Conversion costs:** upfront expenses for switching currencies (e.g. modifying pricing systems)
Stability in exchange rates: absence of currency fluctuations can make long-term business planning and investment more attractive	**Loss of monetary autonomy:** individual countries give up control over key policies like interest rates and inflation targeting

WTO vs. trading bloc conflicts:
- The WTO oversees global trade by encouraging the liberalisation of trade through negotiations and agreements, and acting as a mediator in trade conflicts between member nations.
- WTO promotes open global trade, whereas trading blocs often favour internal trade and can impose restrictions on outsiders. This contradiction can undermine WTO objectives.
- However, trading blocs may also stimulate wider trade liberalisation by simplifying negotiations between larger, unified entities.

Restrictions on free trade

Countries limit free trade to protect their own interests, often to shield vulnerable industries or maintain economic stability.

- **Reasons for restrictions on trade:**
  - **Infant industries:** protect new businesses that can't yet compete globally.
  - **Sunset industries:** support declining sectors to prevent sudden job losses and economic disruption.
  - **Employment:** safeguard jobs from outsourcing or structural unemployment.
  - **Current account deficits:** address imbalances from importing more than exporting.
- **Types of protectionism:**
  - **Tariffs:** taxes on imports that raise prices, protect domestic producers, reduce imports and can increase domestic employment.

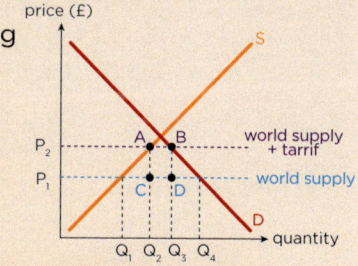

	Before tariff	After tariff
Consumer prices	P1	P2
Domestic output	Q1	Q3
Imports	Q1Q3	Q3Q4
Tax revenue	0	ABCD
Welfare loss	0	ACE and BDF

  - **Quotas:** limits on import quantities that raise prices and protect domestic producers but can cause shortages.
  - **Subsidies:** financial aid to domestic firms, lowering production costs, boosting output and improving export competitiveness.

	Before subsidy	After subsidy
Consumer price	P1	P1
Domestic output	A	B
Imports	AC	BC

  - **Non-tariff barriers:** regulations that indirectly restrict imports by making it harder for foreign producers to sell in the domestic market.
- **Impacts of protectionism:**
  - **Consumers:** higher prices, less choice and reduced living standards.
  - **Producers:** benefit through higher revenues and increased output.
  - **Government:** gain tariff revenue but may incur subsidy costs.
  - **Equality:** helps domestic workers but may worsen conditions for foreign producers and consumers.

International economics

Balance of payments

The balance of payments records all financial transactions between a country and the rest of the world over a period.

Components of the balance of payments:
- **Current account:** tracks the flow of goods, services, investment incomes, and transfers:
  - **Trade in goods balance:** difference between value of goods exported and value of goods imported.
  - **Trade in services balance:** difference between value of services exported and value of services imported.
  - **Primary income balance (investment income):** income received from overseas assets owned by residents minus income paid to foreign owners of assets in the UK.
  - **Secondary income balance (current transfers):** payments received from foreign governments and institutions minus payments sent abroad (e.g. foreign aid).
- **Capital and financial account:** records the ownership changes in financial assets between the UK and other countries:
  - **Foreign Direct Investment (FDI):** net investment by foreign firms into the UK minus UK firms' investments abroad.
  - **Portfolio investment:** net purchase of shares and bonds by foreigners in the UK minus UK residents' purchases abroad.
  - **Short-term capital flows:** net 'hot money' movements, or quick capital inflows and outflows between the UK and other countries.
  - **Changes in foreign currency reserves:** adjustments made by the government or central bank to currency reserves.
- The total of these components makes up the current account balance.
  - **Negative value (−):** indicates current account deficit.
  - **Positive value (+):** indicates current account surplus.

- **Causes of current account deficits:**
  - **Low productivity:** UK goods and services may be less efficient or more costly than foreign competitors.
  - **Offshoring of manufacturing:** many production activities have moved to countries with lower labour costs.
  - **Appreciation of currency:** a stronger exchange rate makes imports cheaper and exports more expensive.
  - **Sustained economic growth:** increased demand often leads to higher imports.
- **Causes of current account surpluses:** these are essentially the opposite of deficit causes:
  - High productivity
  - Competitive manufacturing base
  - Depreciation or weaker exchange rate
  - Slower economic growth reducing import demand
- **Measures to reduce a current account imbalance:**
  - Expenditure-reducing policies: aim to lower demand in the economy → reducing import spending. Includes contractionary fiscal policies and tight monetary policies.
  - Expenditure-switching policies: designed to shift spending from imported goods to domestically produced goods.
  - Devaluation/depreciation: lowering value of currency to make exports cheaper and imports more expensive → improving the trade balance.
- **Significance of global trade imbalances:**
  - **Problems with persistent deficits:**
    - Suggest a country's goods and services lack competitiveness internationally.
    - Could lead to rising unemployment if domestic industries decline.
  - **When deficits might be less concerning:**
    - If caused by importing capital goods, which could boost future productivity.
    - If it is short term.
    - If financed easily by capital inflows recorded in the financial account.
  - **Issues with persistent surpluses:**
    - Could cause inflation by increasing aggregate demand.
    - Might indicate falling living standards if fewer goods are available domestically.
    - May result in currency appreciation → making exports less competitive

International economics

Exchange rates

The exchange rate is the value of one currency expressed in terms of another currency.

- **Exchange rate systems:**
  - **Floating exchange rate:** currency's value is determined by supply and demand in the foreign exchange market.
  - **Fixed exchange rate:** country's currency is fixed against another currency or a basket of currencies.
  - **Managed exchange rate:** currency floats freely but central bank can occasionally intervene in the foreign exchange market to influence its value.
- **Effects on currency:**
  - **Revaluation:** an increase in the value of a currency within a fixed exchange rate system.
  - **Appreciation:** a rise in the currency's value under a floating exchange rate system.
  - **Devaluation:** a reduction in the value of a currency within a fixed exchange rate system.
  - **Depreciation:** a fall in the currency's value under a floating exchange rate system.
- **Factors affecting floating exchange rates:**
  - **Relative inflation rates:** if a country experiences higher inflation than its trading partners → currency's purchasing power declines relative to others → leads to depreciation over time.
  - **Relative interest rates:** higher interest rates compared to other countries can attract foreign capital → increasing demand for the currency → causing it to appreciate.
  - **Current account balance:** rising current account deficit → more of the country's currency is supplied on international markets relative to demand → resulting in depreciation.
- **Government intervention in currency markets:**
  - **Foreign currency transactions:** reduce the value of currency → central bank might sell its own currency on the foreign exchange market → increases supply → currency's value falls.
  - **Interest rate policy:** lowering base interest rate → discourage foreign investment → increasing supply of currency on international markets → reducing its value.

- **Competitive devaluation/depreciation:**
  - Countries can deliberately depreciate their currency to boost economic growth by making exports more competitive.
  - However, this can provoke retaliation leading to a 'currency war.' This is when multiple countries competitively devalue their currencies. These often encourage protectionist policies, undermining global trade.
- **Impact of changes in exchange rates:**
  - **Current account of the balance of payments:** devaluation or depreciation tends to lower foreign currency price of exports and increase the domestic price of imports.
    - This enhances the competitiveness of domestic goods and services → improving current account balance.
    - This improvement only occurs if the **Marshall-Lerner condition** is satisfied: the combined price elasticity of demand for exports and imports must be less than –1.
    - Additionally, the **J-curve effect** explains that immediately after a depreciation, the trade balance may initially worsen (X) before improving over time (Y).
  - **Economic growth and employment:** by improving net exports → depreciation can raise AD → increases real output → leads to higher employment → lower unemployment rates.
  - **Inflation rate:** increased cost of imported raw materials and goods → push production costs up → resulting in cost-push inflation. Higher AD caused by improved net exports → adds to inflationary pressures.
  - **Foreign Direct Investment (FDI) flows:** weaker currency → investment cheaper for foreign companies → encouraging higher levels of inward FDI.

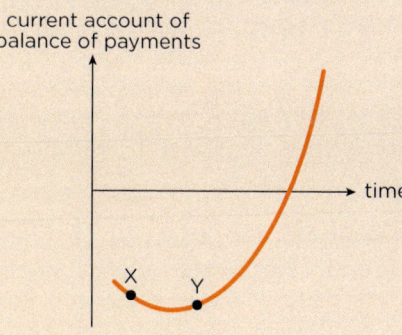

Poverty and inequality

International competitiveness

International competitiveness is the ability of a country's goods and services to compete effectively in global markets. Usually measured through relative costs and prices of exports compared to other countries.

- **Measures of international competitiveness:**
  - **Relative unit labour costs:** calculates average cost of labour per unit of output. Lower value indicates higher competitiveness.
  - **Relative export prices:** compares a country's export prices to those of key international competitors. Lower relative export prices can make a country's goods more attractive abroad.
- **Factors influencing international competitiveness**
  - **Unit labour costs:** if labour costs rise faster than productivity → overall competitiveness declines. Efficient and low-cost labour helps keep exports competitively priced.
  - **Government laws and regulations:** environmental rules, OH&S, and labour laws can impact production costs, influencing competitiveness.
  - **Research and development (R&D):** investment in R&D leads to innovation, improved technology/productivity and competitiveness.
- **Advantages:** improved current account balance means stronger exports that can reduce trade deficits, and economic growth means increased net exports, raising aggregate demand and triggering multiplier effects.
- **Disadvantages:** rise in unemployment in less competitive domestic industries, and currency depreciation → foreign goods more expensive.

Absolute and relative poverty
All specs except: CCEA

- **Absolute poverty:** occurs when individuals lack sufficient income or resources to meet the minimum standard of living necessary for survival, including essentials such as adequate food, shelter, clothing, access to clean water (e.g. a person living on less than $1.90 per day = poverty line).
- **Relative poverty:** defined in relation to standard of living and income levels within a specific country. This reflects economic inequality and social exclusion rather than just survival. An individual is in relative poverty if their income falls below a certain threshold compared to the average or median income in their country (e.g. in the EU, less than 60% of median income).
- **Causes of changes in absolute and relative poverty:**
  - **Unemployment levels:** high unemployment reduces household incomes, potentially pushing individuals below poverty line.
  - **Access to education and healthcare:** lack of access limits opportunities for upward mobility, keeping individuals trapped in poverty.
  - **Availability of public services:** strong public services can alleviate the effects of poverty, while weak infrastructure can worsen it.

Inequality
All specs except: CCEA

- **Wealth:** stock of assets owned by an individual or household at a point in time. Wealth inequality reflects differences in the value of these assets among individuals.
- **Income:** flow concept representing earnings received over a period. Income inequality refers to unequal distribution of these earnings between individuals or households. Measures of income inequality include:
  - **Lorenz Curve:** graphical representation showing proportion of total income earned by cumulative percentages of the population. The further the curve is from the line of perfect equality, the greater the inequality.
  - **Gini coefficient:** numerical measure derived from the Lorenz Curve.

  $$G = \frac{A}{A+B}$$

  - A is the area between the line of equality and the Lorenz Curve.
  - B is the area under the Lorenz Curve.
  - Gini coefficient of 0 = perfect equality, 1 = perfect inequality.
- **Causes of income and wealth inequality:**
  - **Within countries:**
    - **Globalisation:** increases earnings for high-skilled workers and capital owners but may suppress wages in low-skilled sectors.
    - **Differences in education and skill levels:** higher education tends to correlate with higher income.
  - **Between countries:**
    - **Natural resources:** countries rich in resources may generate more wealth, but it depends on how resources are managed.
    - **Political stability:** countries with stable institutions attract more investment and can deliver consistent economic growth.
- **Impact of economic change and development on inequality:**
  - **Kuznets curve:** diagram showing that as an economy develops inequality initially increases due to industrialisation and capital accumulation. Over time, it decreases as wealth is redistributed via policies, education, and rising living standards.
- **Significance of capitalism for inequality:** in a capitalist economy, there is a division between owners of capital and workers. Owners receive profits and dividends, accumulating more wealth over time than wage earners, meaning inequality increases. Without progressive taxation or redistributive policies, capitalism can exacerbate both income and wealth inequality.

Emerging and developing economies

Measures of development

- **Human Development Index (HDI):** composite indicator created by UN to assess country's social and economic development. HDI is made up of three key components:
  - **Living standards:** measured using **GNI per capita** adjusted for purchasing power parity (PPP), which accounts for differences in the cost of living between countries. This reflects average income and purchasing power.
  - **Health:** measured using **life expectancy at birth.** This acts as a proxy for overall health conditions and healthcare quality.
  - **Education:** calculated using **mean years of schooling** and **expected years of schooling.**

Advantages	Disadvantages
Enables meaningful cross-country comparisons	Averages can hide inequalities within countries
Offers more comprehensive view of development compared to just GDP per capita	Still limited as it only considered three aspects of development
Uses widely available, quantifiable data indicators	Developing countries may have poor quality/outdated data

Other metrics that are considered:
- **Inequality-adjusted HDI (IHDI):** adjusts HDI based on distributional inequality across its dimensions.
- **Multidimensional Poverty Index (MPI):** measures deprivation in education, health, and standard of living across multiple indicators.
- **Gender Inequality Index (GII):** captures gender-based disparities in health, empowerment, and labour market participation.
- **Infant mortality rate and maternal mortality ratio:** health-focused indicators that reflect healthcare access and quality.
- **Literacy rates or school enrolment ratios:** Education indicators showing access and attainment.
- **Access to clean water and sanitation:** infrastructure-related development indicators.
- **Internet access:** percentage of population with access to the internet (reflects digital inclusion and access to information).
- **Civil rights and freedoms:** percentage of people entitled to basic civil rights (freedom of speech, political participation etc).

Factors influencing growth and development

- **Primary product dependency and volatility of commodity prices:** many emerging and developing nations heavily rely on exporting primary commodities. This creates economic vulnerability due to:
  - **Large price swings:** both demand and supply for these goods tend to be price inelastic, so small shifts in global conditions can cause major price fluctuations.
  - **Domestic shortages:** when countries prioritise exporting cash crops, there is insufficient food or raw materials left for local use.
  - **Currency appreciation:** rise in global demand for a specific export can increase demand for that country's currency, making other exports less competitive.
  - **Prebisch-Singer hypothesis:** suggests that over time, terms of trade worsen for countries dependent on primary goods. As incomes grow globally, demand for manufactured goods increases more rapidly than for primary goods. Developing countries earn less relative to imports.
- **Savings Gap – Harrod-Domar Model:** low-income countries tend to have low savings rates, limiting their ability to invest in capital and infrastructure.
- **Foreign currency gap:** developing countries may struggle to get enough foreign currency due to over-reliance on primary exports, dependence on costly imports, or capital flight (when people move money abroad).

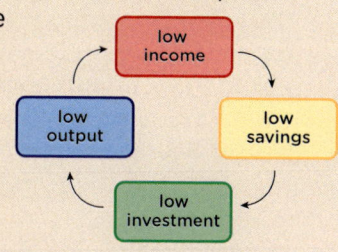

- **Demographics factors:** in countries where population growth > GDP growth, income per capita falls. An ageing population can strain public finances (fewer workers must support a growing number of retirees).
- **Debt:** high levels of external debt can arise from falling currency (debt repayments become more expensive), poor terms of trade from reliance on primary exports, or debt burdens reducing resources available for public investment in health, education, and infrastructure.
- **Access to finance:** limited access to credit and banking services makes it difficult for entrepreneurs to start businesses or for firms to grow, restricting economic development.
- **Infrastructure:** good infrastructure is essential for economic activity. Weak infrastructure discourages domestic investment and foreign direct investment (FDI).
- **Education and skills:** if enrolment and completion rates are low, it leads to a poorly skilled workforce, reducing productivity, discouraging FDI, and limiting innovation and adaptability.

Emerging and developing economies

Strategies influencing growth and development

- **Market-oriented strategies:** aim to reduce government intervention and rely on free markets to drive growth.
  - **Trade liberalisation:** removal of trade barriers, increasing trade, competition, efficiency, and consumer choice.
    - At P_1 (original price), domestic supply is Q_1.
    - Imports are Q_1Q_2.
    - After removal of trade barriers, price falls to P_2.
    - Domestic supply falls to Q_3.
    - Imports increase to Q_3Q_4.

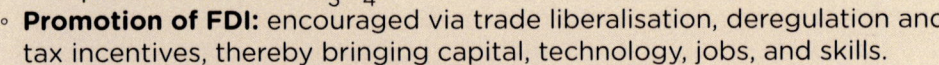

  - **Promotion of FDI:** encouraged via trade liberalisation, deregulation and tax incentives, thereby bringing capital, technology, jobs, and skills.
  - **Removal of government subsidies:** removes market distortions and encourages efficiency and competition.
  - **Floating exchange rate systems:** currency value is determined by market. This means depreciation can boost export competitiveness.
  - **Microfinance schemes:** provides small loans to the poor for business ventures. However, high interest rates on repayments may allow for exploitation.
  - **Privatisation:** transfers firms to private ownership. This assumes that competition and profit motive help to improve efficiency.
- **Interventionist strategies:** involve government action to stimulate development:
  - **Development of human capital:** investment in education and training, improving productivity and attracting FDI.
  - **Protectionism:** tariffs, quotas and subsidies are applied to protect domestic industries, encouraging local production and infant industry growth.
  - **Managed exchange rates:** the central bank can intervene to influence currency value (e.g. depreciating currency to boost exports).
  - **Infrastructure development:** roads, electricity, water, internet. This is important for private sector growth and FDI.
  - **Promoting joint ventures:** foreign and local firms share ownership and operations, allowing for technology and knowledge transfer.
  - **Buffer stock schemes:** stabilises prices of volatile commodities.
    - When equilibrium price is P_1, no action required by the government as it is within the allowed price range.
    - If supply is S_1, price range falls below floor price.
    - Quantity CD is removed from market and stored in buffer stock.
    - If supply falls to S_3, the government will stop prices rising above ceiling price level by releasing quantity AB from buffer stock.

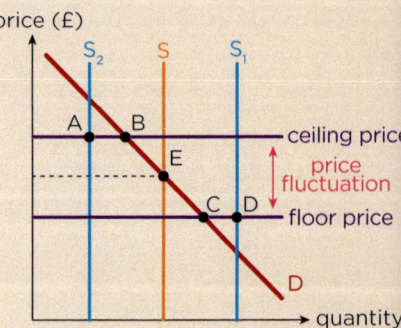

- **Other strategies:**
  - **Industrialisation – The Lewis Model:**
    - Dual-sector economy: traditional agriculture (low productivity, surplus labour) and modern industry (high productivity).
    - Surplus labour shifts to industry at low opportunity cost.
    - Requires investment in industrial capital.
  - **Development of tourism:** brings in tax revenue and creates jobs, but can lead to overdependence or environmental degradation.
  - **Development of primary industries:** effective if demand is income elastic and the country has a comparative advantage (e.g. growth from agriculture, oil, mineral extraction, etc.).
  - **Fair Trade schemes:** ensure a fair price for producers and enables investment in quality. However, the money available for development is small, and this may exclude poor farmers outside the scheme.
  - **Aid:** transfer of resources to promote development. This reduces absolute poverty and inequality, filling the saving gap. However, it is subject to exploitation by corrupt governments.
    - **Tied aid:** requires recipients to buy goods from the donor country
    - **Bilateral aid:** from one country to another
    - **Multilateral aid:** through NGOs like World Bank
  - **Debt relief:** cancelling or rescheduling loans, increasing business confidence and boosting investment, though with a risk of moral hazard
  - **International institutions:**
    - **World Bank:** provides long-term loans and expertise for development.
    - **International Monetary Fund (IMF):** ensures global monetary cooperation by offering loans for balance of payments deficits.
    - **Non-Government Organisations (NGOs):** independent, non-profit organisations that provide community-based development.

The financial sector and state role in macroeconomy

The financial sector
- **Role of financial markets**
  - **To facilitate saving:** let people and businesses save money securely.
  - **To lend to businesses and individuals:** e.g. mortgages and loans.
  - **To facilitate exchange of goods and services:** support everyday payments for smooth functioning of domestic/international economies.
  - **To provide forward markets in currencies and commodities:** where contracts are made now for transactions that occur in the future. This is used for **hedging** (protecting against future price changes) and **speculation** (attempting to profit from price changes).
  - **To provide a market for equities:** companies issue shares to raise money and buy ownership stakes to earn dividends or capital gains.
- **Market failures in the financial sector**
  - **Asymmetric information:** one party knows less than the other.
  - **Externalities:** risks in finance affect people who aren't directly involved.
  - **Moral hazard:** taking risks knowing they will be bailed out.
  - **Speculation and market bubbles:** investors buy based on 'hype.'
  - **Market rigging:** manipulating prices/info to gain unfair advantage.
- **Role of central banks:**
  - **Implementation of monetary policy:** main tool for controlling inflation and economic stability through **interest rates** and **quantitative easing**.
  - **Banker to the government:** manages accounts and issues debt.
  - **Lender of last resort:** provides emergency funding to banks during a financial crisis or a runs on banks.
  - **Regulating the banking industry:** ensures financial stability and prevents risky practices. The Central Bank's regulatory responsibilities are to set capital requirements, enforce risk management rules, and conduct bank inspections.

National debt
The national debt is the cumulative total of all previous fiscal deficits that have not yet been repaid. Factors affecting the size of national debt include:
- **Recurring fiscal deficits:** persistent annual deficits accumulate into national debt. A surplus in any given year can be used to reduce debt or redirected toward further investment.
- **Government policy choices:** tax and spending decisions have direct effect on debt levels (e.g. cutting corporate taxes during booms reduces revenue and slows debt repayment despite strong economic performance).

Public expenditure
- **Capital expenditure:** government spending on projects and assets intended to deliver long-term benefits.
- **Current expenditure:** routine government spending required for daily operations (e.g. public sector wages, utility bills etc.).
- **Transfer payments:** sums paid by the government to individuals (e.g. unemployment benefits, pensions).
- **Reasons for changing size and composition of global spending:** during economic downturns or crises, governments often boost spending to stimulate demand. Ageing populations also push expenditure on pensions, increasing costs of healthcare and social services.
- **Impacts of public expenditure levels as proportion of GDP on:**
  - **Productivity and growth:** when governments invest in infrastructure, education and healthcare → they contribute to both human and physical capital → enhances productivity → stimulates long-term growth.
  - **Living standards:** government spending on essential services like healthcare, education and housing support → improves quality of life
  - **Crowding out:** if public sector borrowing is too high → may raise interest rates → limited funds for investment → slowing down economic growth.
  - **Level of taxation:** higher levels of public spending requires higher taxes → impacts disposable income, business incentives/consumer behaviour.
  - **Equality:** redistributive policies and welfare programmes → public spending can narrow income gaps by supporting those with lower earnings and improving access to services.

Public sector finances and fiscal deficit
- **Automatic stabilisers:** fiscal mechanisms that respond to changes in the economic cycle without direct government action.
- **Discretionary fiscal policy:** involves deliberate changes to government spending or taxation to influence AD.
- **Fiscal deficit:** when government expenditure > revenue within a specific financial year. Factors influencing the size of fiscal deficits include: **economic conditions** (e.g. during booms → revenue rises → spending decreases) and **housing market performance** (e.g. active market → enhanced public income from property taxes → helps narrow the deficit).
- **Structural deficit:** persists even when the economy is operating at/near full capacity due to underlying imbalances in government income/expenditure.
- **Cyclical deficit:** occurs due to economic downturns. During periods of low economic activity, tax revenues decrease and government spending rises, resulting in a temporary budget deficit. Cyclical deficit typically diminish as the economy recovers.

State role in macroeconomy

Taxation

- **Types of tax systems:**
  - **Progressive tax (P):** tax rates increase as income rises. Those who earn more, pay larger percentage of their income in tax. This is designed to reduce income inequality.
  - **Proportional tax (F):** everyone pays the same percentage of their income. This treats all taxpayers equally in rate but not in impact.
  - **Regressive tax (R):** places a heavier financial burden on those on a low income. They pay higher percentage of their income compared to those on high income.

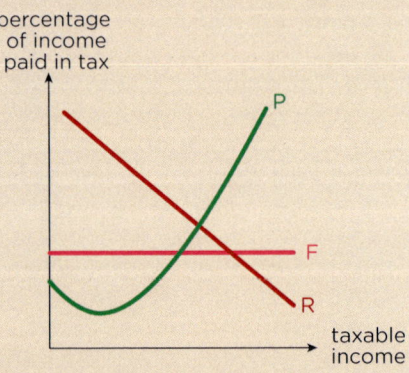

- **Economic effects of changes in tax rates:**
  - **Incentives to work:** if income taxes are too high, it may discourage additional work or reduce motivation to be more productive.
  - **Tax revenues:** the Laffer curve (right) shows the relationship between tax rates and revenue. Initially, increasing tax rates boosts revenue, but after a certain point, it reduces economic activity, ultimately leading to lower tax revenue.

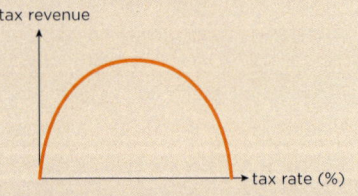

  - **Income distribution:** progressive taxation systems can help rebalance income inequality (by shifting resources from high earners to those in need through public services and benefits).
  - **Real output and employment:** Reducing taxes on businesses and individuals, boosting investment, increasing consumer spending, and leading to job creation, thus stimulating economic output.
  - **Price level:** indirect taxes (e.g. VAT) increase the cost of goods and services, leading to prices increase for consumer and increased inflation.
  - **Trade balance:** taxes on imports reduce demand for foreign goods, improving the trade balance. However, this risks retaliation from trading partners.
  - **FDI flows:** Low corporate tax rates can attract international investors looking for favourable conditions to operate in.

Macroeconomic policies in a global context

- **Policy objectives and approaches:**
  - **Measures to reduce fiscal deficits and national debts:** public debt can support economic growth through investment; however, excessive debt can become problematic. Use of QE has prompted debates about whether governments should rely on borrowing for capital spending or consider money creation. Austerity (used to reduce deficits) can have prolonged social impacts and harm lower income groups much more.
  - **Measures to reduce poverty and inequality:** some countries operate progressive tax systems and then redistribute according to needs. Others complement progressive taxes with universal access to education and healthcare. Policy choices in this area are strongly influenced by political ideologies and value based (normative) economics.
  - **Changes in interest rates and supply of money:** central banks adjust interest rates and money supply mostly based on domestic economic conditions. International developments can force a policy shift (e.g. interest rate increases abroad can pressure a country to follow in order to prevent currency depreciation).
  - **Measures to increase international competitiveness:** protectionist policies, currency devaluation and supply-side policies.
- **Macroeconomic policy responses to global external shocks:**
  - 2008 Global Financial Crisis resulting in some banks nationalised.
  - U.S China Trade War: triggered series of retaliatory trade measures.
  - COVID-19 Pandemic: widespread fiscal and monetary interventions.
  - Russia-Ukraine War: disrupted global food and energy markets (Ukraine's grain exports and Russia's gas supplies).
- **Measures to control transnational operations:** limits to a state's ability to control global companies. This depends on a state's power, the maturity of a country's systems, TNC leverage, and the existence of monopolies.
  - **Regulation of transfer pricing:** corporations create internal subsidiaries to manipulate pricing (e.g. a company might extract resources and sell them to its own subsidiary at an artificially low price, reducing taxable income in the resource-rich country).
- **Problems facing policymakers when applying policies:**
  - **Inaccurate information:** economic data often reflects past trends and may not capture present developments or may be misinterpreted.
  - **Risks and uncertainties:** unpredictable outcomes make it difficult to assess the full implications of a policy. Risks can be underestimated and some uncertainties only emerge after implementation of policies.
  - **Inability to control external shocks:** global events (conflicts, pandemics) have widespread effects that domestic policies often cannot prevent.